Essential
Seville

by

GEORGE KEAN

George Kean is an experienced travel writer who lives and works in Spain. He is the author of three Spanish titles in the current series of *Essential* guides.

D0711995

Produced by AA Publishing

Written by George Kean
Additional research by Jens Poulsen
Peace and Quiet section
by Paul Sterry
Series Adviser: Ingrid Morgan
Series Controller: Nia Williams
Copy editor: Antonia Hebbert

Edited, designed and produced by
AA Publishing. Maps ©
The Automobile Association 1992

Distributed in the United Kingdom
by the Publishing Division of The
Automobile Association, Fanum
House, Basingstoke, Hampshire,
RG21 2EA.

The contents of this publication are
believed correct at the time of
printing. Nevertheless, the
publishers cannot accept
responsibility for errors or
omissions, nor for changes in details
given. We have tried to ensure
accuracy in this guide, but things do
change and we would be grateful if
readers could advise us of any
inaccuracies they may encounter.

A CIP catalogue record for this book
is available from the British Library.

ISBN 0 7495 0317 3

Published by The Automobile
Association

Typesetting: Tradespools Ltd,
Frome, Somerset

Colour separation: Mullis Morgan
Ltd, London

Printed in Italy by Printers SRL,
Trento

Front cover picture: Plaza de España

This book employs a
simple rating system to
help choose which
places to visit.

 do not miss

 see if you can

◆ worth seeing if
you have time

INTRODUCTION

Through the centuries, scribes and chroniclers, including today's travel writers, have overused the word beautiful and all its synonyms in describing Seville (Sevilla). They had no option: much of the central city is just that, very beautiful indeed. It is crowded with a wealth of Gothic, Mudéjar, Renaissance and baroque architecture. But it is not only the fine buildings and attractive urban arrangement which provoke appreciation. It is also the city's *alegría*, a vital spark to making the most of the present, the dark good looks of the Sevillanos and their *gracia*, a graciousness supported by good humour and an ever-present desire to have fun. Seville is a city of extreme contrasts. In its streets the sour odour of horse droppings and urine mingle with the sweet smell of orange trees. The multi-coloured, elaborate decoration of the medieval Reales Alcázares contrasts with the colourless sleekness of high-tech buildings raised for Expo'92. The solemnity of its Semana Santa observance contrasts with the frivolous abandonment and self-indulgence during the Feria de Abril two weeks later; in its music—flamenco—the haunting singing called *cante jondo* is often an outcry against injustice, but contrasts with the light and joyful *cante chico* of the fashionable *sevillanas*. The wealth of great landowning families contrasts with the abjectness of beggars, illiterates and the many unemployed; and those interested in the political scene will also find a complicated picture with its own share of ambiguities. Expo'92 has put Seville at the centre of world attention, but it has been there before. When Spain was at its most powerful in the 15th and 16th centuries, Seville had the world's busiest port and was one of its four largest cities. For 214 years it held the monopoly of Spain's trade with its far-flung colonies. In life and death, Cristóbal Colón (Christopher Columbus) had a very special relationship with the monastery of La Cartuja, the historical centrepiece of Expo'92. *Victoria*, the first ship to circumnavigate the globe, left from the city, sailing some 72 miles (115 km) down the Río Guadalquivir to the open Atlantic. Amerigo Vespucci, who was to give his name to the American continents, sailed from a wharf on the river. Further back in Seville's potent pedigree, myth claims Hercules as the founder of the city and history confirms that

Grand Moorish-style pavilions built for the 1929 Ibero-América Exhibition still grace the Parque de María Luisa

Julius Caesar surrounded it with protective walls. During Spain's cultural Golden Age of the 17th century, Seville contributed the exceptional talents of Velázquez, Murillo and many more. And there is something especially splendid about a city which can inspire and be the setting of operas like *Carmen, Don Giovanni* and *The Barber of Seville.*

In 1929 Seville hosted the Ibero-América Exhibition. Its legacy was some enhancement of the inner city and a number of large buildings, many of which are now used as museums and cultural venues. The legacy of Expo'92 will be very much greater. There has been a massive infrastructural improvement in and around the city and the rest of Andalucía. Historic buildings and monuments have been renovated, and, impressive new cultural venues have been built in the city and on La Cartuja island.

Accommodation has greatly increased in quality and quantity, and the Expo'92 site should become an important centre for research and technological progress. In short, the city has received a massive boost to launch it into the next century.

Beguiling, romantic, historic, modern and futuristic, Seville offers one of the world's most rewarding travel experiences. And there is more: Seville is capital of Andalucía, one of Spain's 17 autonomous regions and, by any judgement, a fascinating region. It has the largest percentage of land area designated as natural reserves within Europe, contrasting with tightly packed ribbon development along its Costa del Sol. Snow-capped mountains overlook extensive and rich agricultural plains; areas of semi-desert contrast with those of very high rainfall and luxuriant growth. Seville is challenged in beauty and interest for visitors by Córdoba and Granada. Their grandeur, and that of many towns, contrasts with hundreds of humble, whitewashed *pueblos* (villages) throughout Andalucía's eight provinces.

With increased and improved air, rail and road access, Seville is now the ideal gateway for discovering Andalucía and, within the region, new roads have reduced journey times. Be assured that you will be enchanted by Seville, Andalucía and the Andaluz people.

BACKGROUND

Seville's origins stretch back to neolithic times,
when there is evidence that Carmona, just east
of the city, was a large settlement. After 1500BC,
new settlers arrived, probably from North
Africa, and are now known as the Iberians. By
1000BC, the rich but mysterious state of Tartessos
had been established in the area. The Río Tinto
district was rich in ores which the Tartessians
mined and traded with Phoenicians and, later,
with Greeks, who had colonies along Iberia's
Mediterranean coastline. Tartessos was
conquered by Carthaginians from North Africa,
who gave the name of Hispalis to their
settlement on the site of today's Seville. When
they fought with Rome in the Punic Wars of the
3rd century BC, southern Iberia (now Andalucía)
saw much of the fighting. The Roman Scipio
Africanus had a decisive victory over
Hasdrubal's Carthaginian forces at Carmona in
206BC. He began building Itálica, just north of
Hispalis, which became a town of some
importance and splendour and was to produce
two Roman Emperors. For the next 600 years the
Romans imposed their sovereignty over their
new province, which they at first named
Hispanis Ulterior. They began building
aqueducts, roads and cities, remnants of which
remain in Andalucía, and their language, legal
and civil codes became the base for those now
existing in Spain.
Christianity filtered in during the 1st century.
Justa and Rufina, two Christian sisters from
Seville's Triana district, died in prison for
refusing to yield their virginity in the worship of
Venus, and are honoured as patron saints of the
city. In AD306 all Roman citizens gained religious
freedom. Over the following years, Rome's
empire slowly disintegrated, and in 475 Rome
conceded that the Visigoths (who were Arian
Christians) were rulers of what had been its
Iberian provinces. Seville was the Visigoths'
capital for a time and it was here that the first
Visigothic martyrdom for Catholicism occurred:
in 585 the king had his son, Hermenegildo,
murdered for espousing it. Five years later
Catholicism became the state religion. Sevillan
scholars, San Leandro and San Ildefonso,

Delicate Mudéjar details make the Salón de Embajadores, or Ambassadors' Hall, the centrepiece of the Reales Alcázares

became known far and wide. The Visigoths took up much that was Roman and their legal code, *Fuero Juzgo*, was based on Roman law. Their numbers were few however, and constant rivalry among their military aristocracy and elected monarchy undermined their rule. In 711, it was broken by their defeat in battle on the banks of the Río Guadalete by the army of the Moors, led by Tarik. The Moors were Muslims from North Africa. They captured Seville in 712, and had a ruling presence for the next 780 years in what they named *Al-Andalus*.

For the Moors this was a land of milk and honey to which they contributed their greater learning, advanced administration, knowledge about agriculture and finer architecture. They also implanted their racial stock, religious norms and culture. It is the legacy of the long Moorish presence in the region which today distinguishes Andalucians from other Spaniards: you can see it in people's features, their behaviour and the style of their *pueblos* (villages). In 756, Abderraman I established himself as emir in Córdoba. Jews and Christians could choose between converting to Islam or practising their faiths on payment of taxes. Christians who did not convert were known as *Mozárabes*; those who did were *Muladies* or *Renegados*. Abderraman III raised himself to the status of caliph in 929 and consolidated Muslim rule in the peninsula. Córdoba became Western Europe's most advanced and cultured city, and Seville was regarded as a rich and beautiful city by writers of the time. Almansur, a military strongman during the reign of weak Hisham II, conducted *aceifas* (campaigns) against slowly strengthening Christian kingdoms in the north of the peninsula. When he died in 1002 the caliphate began its decline. Hisham III, the last caliph, abdicated in 1031, and Muslim Spain split into 26 *taifas* (small kingdoms). Some warred with each other, some made pacts with Christian rulers in the north, others consolidated. The most powerful were the kingdoms of Seville and Granada, the former gaining in beauty and importance under its learned and cultured king, Al-Motamid (1069–95). After the loss to the Christians of Toledo in 1085, some taifas asked the Almoravid emir in North Africa for help.

From 1090, the Almoravides began uniting the taifas and imposing a strict religious order which included the persecution of Christians and Jews. Their rivals in North Africa, the Almohades, arrived in Al Andalus in 1147 and by 1170 had replaced the Almoravides. They improved the economy and were keen builders, and, initially, they offered religious freedom. Seville, their capital, received special attention: the Giralda and Torre del Oro are the most prominent reminders of their brief but influential presence. After their defeat in 1212 by the Christian forces of Castile, the Muslims again split into factions, unwittingly helping the Christian Reconquest of Spain.

The Christian king Fernando III took Córdoba from the Moors in 1236 and Seville in 1248, when he rode his horse up the ramp on the inside of the Giralda. This very religious man, *el Santo* (the Saint), made Seville the capital for the remaining four years of his life. His remains, and those of his wife and son Alfonso X, *el Sabio* (the Wise) lie in Seville's great cathedral. Eager to consolidate the Christian faith, Fernando began building churches, in which the architectural styles of northern regions were combined with Moorish architecture to produce the Gothic-Mudéjar style known as *fernandine*. Pedro I was a scheming, murderous womaniser known as *el Cruel*, but he left the fantasy, filigreed palace within the Reales Alcázares which now so delights visitors to Seville.

Territory won from the Moors was divided among the nobility, church and military orders. This created the *latifundios* (large estates) and ruling families whose existence was to cause so much socio-economic damage in the region up to the present time. Muslims remaining in Christian territories were known as *Mudéjares*—hence the term Mudéjar for Muslim craftsmanship and architecture carried out under Christian rule. Those who converted were called *Moriscos*. Jews were forced to live in *juderías* (enclosed city districts). In the 13th century they started arriving in Seville from Toledo and other cities. The judería adjoined the Reales Alcázares of the kings, under whose protection the Jews lived and whom many of them served. Now known as the Barrio de Santa

La Giralda, 12th-century minaret is now the cathedral bell-tower

Cruz, it is one of the city's most evocative quarters.

The last Moorish kingdom was Granada, which was finally defeated by Fernando II of Aragón and Isabela I of Castile (*los Reyes Católicos*—the Catholic Monarchs). They had married in 1469 and had their campaign against the Moors blessed by the Pope as a Holy Crusade, instituting the ruthless Inquisition to root out heretics. Much of their time was spent in Seville's Reales Alcázares, where they planned their assaults on Granada. On 2 January 1492, King Boabdil of Granada gave them the keys of his city. Ferdinand and Isabel had promised him that his people could live peacefully practising their beliefs and customs. It was not a promise they kept.

Cristóbal Colón (Christopher Columbus) returned to Spain in 1493 with news that he had reached the New World. It was a Sevillan,

BACKGROUND

Palacio de San Telmo—a horse-drawn carriage ride is the easiest way to get the feel of the city and its buildings

Rodrigo de Triana, who had first sighted land. Spain started hauling back the treasures of the vast areas it conquered and in 1503 Seville was awarded the Casa de Contratación, by which it monopolised 'trade' with the New World. In August 1519, Fernando de Magallanes set sail from Las Mugus quay in Seville with a fleet of four ships to find a westward route to the Moluccas spice islands. Only the good ship *Victoria*, under the command of Juan Sebastián Elcano, returned to Spain. The first ship to circumnavigate the world had sailed 46,270 miles (74,000 km). The expedition of Amerigo Vespucci, who gave his name to the continent, was also prepared along Seville's river, the Río Guadalquivir.

Seville became very rich as the world's busiest

port and grew to be among its four largest cities.
Grand Renaissance buildings were
commissioned here as elsewhere in Spain, in an
extravagant display of wealth, but in fact the
country was declining. The defeat of Felipe II's
Armada by the English in 1588 was a devastating
personal blow to the king, and signalled the
waning of Spain's unmatched power in the
world. Religious fanaticism did nothing to help:
with the expulsion of Jews and Muslims, the
subjugation and then final expulsion of Moriscos
(1609), Andalucía's productivity progressively
declined. Many Spanish people left to settle in
the New World, and in 1649 a virulent plague
decimated Seville's population. Throughout the
17th century, Spain weakened politically, but
culture flourished in what is called the *Siglo de
Oro*, or Golden Age. Baroque was the dominant
architectural style, and there was a wealth of
talent in Seville to give it exuberant expression,
leaving a treasured legacy of architecture,
painting and sculpture at which visitors to the
city can marvel today. Pachego, Velázquez,
Murillo, Zurbarán, Valdés Leál, Alonso Cano,
Montañes, Juan de Mesa, Roldón and a host of
other artistic talents, including writers and poets,
contributed to the city's creative splendour.
Seville's decline was confirmed when it lost the
Casa de Contratación to Cádiz in 1717. Silting of
the Río Guadalquivir was a constant problem,
and facilities at Cádiz had been improved.
When trade with the Americas was completely
liberalised in 1778, Seville suffered even more.
Sporadic wars with Britain, and the loss of
American colonies, followed until Britain's
victory at the Battle of Trafalgar (Cádiz province)
in 1805. Three years later and up until 1814,
Britain was Spain's ally in the Peninsular War
against Napoleon's forces, whose policy of
destroying or looting architectural and artistic
treasures caused great losses in Seville and
throughout Andalucía. The 19th century was
marked by continuous political upheaval,
including the two-year period of the First
Republic, enthusiastically supported by Seville.
By 1898 Spain had lost all of its colonial empire
after its war with the US, but there was an
intellectual revitalisation led by the group
known as the Generation of '98.

Andalucía had movements for agrarian reform, but they were usually ruthlessly suppressed. There was also a campaign for Andalucian nationalism, led by Blas Infante.

Political and economic stagnation continued into the 20th century, with another cultural revival by the so-called Generation of '27, among whom the poet García Lorca from Granada was a leading light. With the support of King Alfonso XIII, the dictator General Primo de Rivera ran the country between 1923 and 1930, but then resigned. The king abdicated and went into exile soon afterwards.

The majority in Seville and the rest of Andalucía strongly supported the socialists who won the elections of 1931, but again the country could not pull itself out of political chaos. In July 1936, army factions, so-called Nationalists later led by General Franco, rose against the Popular Front government. Control of Seville was taken by General Queipo de Llano in July 1936 and Franco had his headquarters in the city for a time. The ensuing Civil War lasted until early 1939, and each village, town and city has its sad and separate story of the horrors, though Seville itself came through relatively unscathed. Franco, *el Caudillo* (the Leader), ran the country until his death in 1975. Andalucía was not his favourite place and the region received little benevolence from a man who saw himself as a kind father of the people.

From 1975 onwards King Juan Carlos I helped nurture the country peacefully back to democracy, and the royal family is widely popular. Felipe González, President of the Government (Prime Minister) since 1983, comes from Seville, where he first began his clandestine support and work for the PSOE (Socialist Party) during the dark Franco years.

1992 and Beyond
Felipe, as he is popularly known, has enjoyed a powerful position as leader of his party and president of the government. Other members of the group known as the 'Seville Clan', who modernised and rebuilt the socialist party, have also been prominent in Madrid's corridors of power, often raising the complaint of other Spaniards that this favours Andalucía.

Columbus' discovery of the New World brought gold and silver to Seville, and its greatest age of prosperity

Andalucians counter that they suffer because the central government is afraid to show them any favouritism. Alfonso Guerra, who served as Vice President of the Government from 1983 until his resignation early in 1991, has been personally close to Felipe González since their days as students at Seville's university, and the duo have been called *los hermanos siameses* (Siamese twins). Alfonso Guerra has been the party's main ideologist and the more hardline faction of the party which supports him is at times a thorn in the side of the government. Another member of the 'Seville Clan' and one-time minister in Señor González's government, Manuel Chaves, is now President of the Junta de Andalucía, the region's autonomous government. Seville was chosen to be the capital of Andalucía but Granada was a strong contender for the honour. After the

BACKGROUND

The soaring green canopy of the Parque de María Luisa is a cool oasis from the fierce midday sun of the city

municipal elections of May 1991, Alejandro Rojas-Marco became the new *alcalde* (mayor), with the task of presiding over Expo'92—not just a six-month event, but a catalyst for transforming the region after many decades of neglect. The tranformation continues with Cartuja '93, a project to spark off technological innovation for the region, reusing Expo'92's legacy of infrastructure, buildings and equipment on La Cartuja island.

Andalucía is not the only region of Spain with great goals in sight but, although there is a long way to go, its start has been impressive. Andalucía does have distinct advantages, not least its climate and geographical diversity. Another is the role of Cristóbal Colón the roving Genovese who sailed from its shores and reached the Caribbean, believing he had reached the Indies in 1492. The commemoration of that voyage 500 years ago has been the prime

inspiration for Andalucía's surge of infrastructural improvement and economic development, which might not otherwise have happened at such a spectacular pace. In 1976, during a speech delivered in the Dominican Republic, the island of Colón's first major landfall, King Juan Carlos I sowed the seed of an idea that the quincentenary would be the opportunity to celebrate an International Exhibition. The seed grew into Expo'92, with the 'Age of Discoveries' as its theme, commemorating not only Colón but all areas of human discovery. Seville and Andalucia have been reaping the benefits of a vast investment programme, including $7 billion from the Spanish government. Much of it has gone into the transport and communications infrastructure: a high speed line of 300 miles (482 km) cuts the rail journey time between Madrid and Seville to under three hours; more than 620 miles (1,000 km) of dual carriageways have been constructed to facilitate road transport within the region and improve its links with the European road network; airport capacity at Seville has been increased three times, that at Málaga has doubled and at Jerez capacity has also increased; in the area of telecommunications the region will have an advance of 15 years, with a digital network infrastructure connected with fibre optics. Seville has been surrounded by a high-speed ring road, its main roads have been improved, a new railway station replaces two old ones and lines through the city have been eliminated or replaced to modernise the system, the riversides of the Guadalquivir have been enhanced and seven new bridges cross the river. As in other Andalucian towns and cities, many historic buildings in and around Seville have been restored and refurbished. The European Community has generously supported the region's Development Programme, which includes aid for improving the productivity of traditional and new activities in its agricultural and fishery sectors. Private initiatives have been encouraged. Private enterprise has been responsible for greatly extending and improving the quality of hotel accommodation in Seville and other centres. Public and private funds have been directed at improving the cultural environment by providing more and better venues, and better funding of the arts. At the human level, directly and indirectly some 200,000 new jobs have been created.

It is now quite clearly time to begin shaking out memories of Andalucía as a region in limbo between Africa and Europe, where people lived for the pleasure of the present and had little to show off but glories of the past. It is a region of great vitality and timeless inactivity, bewildering contrasts and great strides of material progress. A respect for its cultural heritage remains intact, and has in fact increased. There is an awareness of the need to protect the natural heritage in the face of accumulating economic development, and the hope must be that the awareness generates effective action.

Orientation

Seville is situated only 30 feet (9 m) above sea level and some 72 miles (115 km) upstream from the Atlantic Ocean along the Río Guadalquivir. To the north is the Sierra Morena mountain range, separating Andalucía from Extremadura and Castilla-La Mancha; to the southeast, the western end of the Sistema Bética, behind which is the Costa del Sol of the Mediterranean Sea. The flat plain of the Guadalquivir stretches eastwards and includes Seville province's rich agricultural area of La Campina, which is studded with showpiece towns. Southwest of the city are the marshlands of the Guadalquivir's big estuary, Cádiz province and the fine beaches of the Costa de la Luz.

City Districts

Seville has 24 *barrios*, urban administrative districts. Of most interest to visitors (except for the Expo'92 site) are three barrios on the east bank: Centro, Al Arenal and Santa Cruz. These areas also have most of the best eating places, shops, nightlife venues and hotels. South of the Barrio de Santa Cruz, the Parque María de Luisa and its surroundings is another area of prime interest to visitors. West of Barrio de Santa Cruz, the barrio of Nervion has a number of big hotels and has become a shopping and commercial area of growing interest for visitors. Across the river is the relatively modern barrio of Los Remedios, where the attractions for visitors are

Seville's cathedral is immense, but inside it has surprising delicacy and grace

BACKGROUND

shopping opportunities and nightlife in its many modern music bars. North of here is Triana, whose residents consider themselves as the only real Sevillanos. Visitors come here for a flavour of a traditional residential quarter, now going through a programme of renovation, where there are many typical tapas bars and lower-priced restaurants, as well as crafts and odds-and-ends shops. Across a branch of the Guadalquivir is the manmade island of La Cartuja, not only site of the monastery after which it has been named but also of Expo'92 and, thereafter, of Cartuja 93. New pedestrian and traffic bridges link La Cartuja with the east bank.

Climb to the top of the Giralda, named for its bronze weathervane, for great views across the city rooftops

WHAT TO SEE

Sightseeing highlights are
concentrated within a compact
area on the east bank of the
river. Walking is the best way of
moving from one to the other.
During the hot months, it is
advisable to start seeing the
sights early in the day. This is
also the time, when mass is
being said, that you stand the
best chance of getting into many
of Seville's religious buildings.

Two suggestions for walks which
take in most of the sightseeing
highlights follow the individual
entries below.
Up to four people can hire a
horsedrawn carriage for a
stately ride around the central
sightseeing area. This is an easy
and safe way of getting an initial
feel of the centre, which you can
later explore in more detail.
Agree the price in advance with
the *cochero*. There are carriage
ranks at the Catedral, Torre del

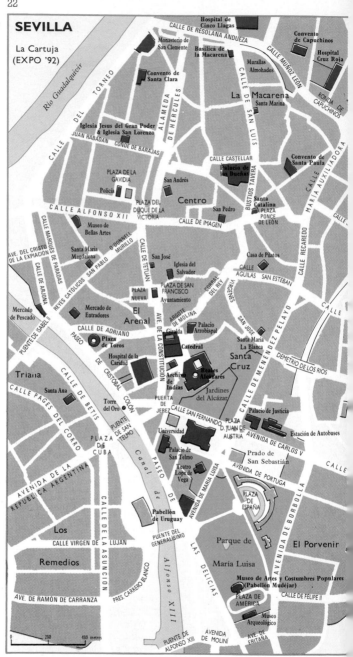

SEVILLA

La Cartuja
(EXPO '92)

Rio Guadalquivir

Hospital de Cinco Llagas
CALLE DE RESOLANA ANDUEZA
Monasterio de San Clemente
Basílica de la Macarena
Convento de Capuchinos
Hospital Cruz Roja
CALLE DE TORNEO
Convento de Santa Clara
Murallas Almohades
La Macarena
Santa Marina
CALLE MUÑIZ LEÓN
RONDA DE CAPUCHINOS
ALAMEDA DE HERCULES
CALLE DE SAN LUIS
Iglesia Jesús del Gran Poder & Iglesia San Lorenzo
JUAN RABADAN
CONDE DE BARAJAS
CALLE CASTELLAR
Convento de Santa Paula
CALLE MARIA AUXILIADORA
PLAZA DE LA GAVIDIA
San Andrés
Palacio de las Dueñas
BUSTIOS TAVERA
CALLE
Policía
Centro
San Pedro
Santa Catalina
PLAZA PONCE DE LEÓN
CALLE RECAREDO
PLAZA DEL DUQUE DE LA VICTORIA
CALLE DE IMAGEN
CALLE ALFONSO XII
Museo de Bellas Artes
Casa de Pilatos
Santa María Magdalena
San José
Iglesia del Salvador
CALLE AGUILAS SAN ESTEBAN
AVE. DEL CRISTO DE LA EXPIACIÓN
O'DONNELL MURILLO
CALLE DE TETUAN
PLAZA DE SAN FRANCISCO
CORRAL DEL REY
VIRGENES
CALLE DE ARJONA
SANTA PABLO
REYES CATÓLICOS
PLAZA NUEVA
Ayuntamiento
ARGOTE DE MOLINA
SAN JOSE
Mercado de Pescado
Mercado de Entradores
El Arenal
Palacio Arzobispal
Santa María La Blanca
CALLE DE MENENDEZ PELAYO
PUENTE DE ISABEL II
CALLE DE ADRIANO
Giralda
Catedral
Santa Cruz
DEMETRIO DE LOS RIOS
Plaza de Toros
PASEO DE CRISTOBAL
Hospital de la Caridad
Reales Alcázares
Triana
CALLE DE BETIS
Santa Ana
Archivo de Indias
Jardines del Alcázar
CALLE PAGES DEL CORRO
Torre del Oro
COLÓN
PUERTA DE JEREZ
Palacio de Justicia
CALLE SAN FERNANDO
PLAZA D. JUAN DE AUSTRIA
Palacio de Justicia
PLAZA DE CUBA
PUENTE DE SAN TELMO
Universidad
Estación de Autobuses
AVENIDA DE LA REPUBLICA ARGENTINA
CALLE DE LUJAN
Palacio de San Telmo
Prado de San Sebastián
AVENIDA DE CARLOS V
AVENIDA DE PORTUGAL
CALLE
Teatro Lope de Vega
AVENIDA DE MARIA LUISA
PLAZA DE ESPAÑA
Los
Pabellón de Uruguay
AVENIDA DE BORBOLLA
CALLE VIRGEN DE LA LUJAN
PUENTE DEL GENERALISIMO
Parque de
El Porvenir
Remedios
Canal de
PASEO DE LAS DELICIAS
María Luisa
PRES CARREIRO BLANCO
Alfonso XIII
AVE. DE RAMÓN DE CARRANZA
Museo de Artes y Costumbres Populares (Pabellón Mudéjar)
PLAZA DE AMÉRICA
CALLE DE FELIPE II
Museo Arqueológico
PUENTE DE ALFONSO XIII
AVENIDA DE MOLINÍ
AVE. DE ERITAÑA

0   200   400 metres

Oro, Plaza de España and Jardines de Murillo.

Another perspective can be gained by taking one of the river cruises of different duration which depart from, and return to, near the Torre del Oro. There are also evening cruises, some with flamenco performances or disco dancing. For information ask hotel porters or tourist offices, or go to the departure point.

Start your planning by getting a map. Those given free by tourist offices are adequate, but you can buy more comprehensive maps at kiosks or bookshops.

Alameda de Hércules

◆
ALAMEDA DE HÉRCULES
This wide and shady avenue in the north of the city has two columns, which were once part of a Roman temple, topped by statues commemorating two important figures in Sevillan mythology and history. Hercules is credited in myth as the founder of the city; Julius Caesar fortified the city by surrounding it with walls in 45BC.

◆◆
ARCHIVO DE LAS INDIAS
Avenida de la Constitución
Felipe II gave the task of designing the *Lonja* (Exchange) to one of his favourite architects, Juan de Herrera, whose sombre style complemented the king's character. The building was completed in 1598 and has served its present purpose from 1758. More than four million documents relating to Spain's connections with the New World are preserved here.
Researchers can now access them by electronic means. One of the galleries has an exhibition of sample material, usually including pages from the diaries or letters of Colón (Columbus).
Open: Monday to Friday 10.00–13.00 hrs.

◆
ATENEO DE SEVILLA
Calle Santo Tomás 5
Various exhibitions, open to the public, are held in the Sala Zurbarán of Seville's literary and artistic 'club'.
Open: usually Monday to Saturday 18.00–21.00 hrs; Sunday and holidays 12.00–14.00 and 18.00–21.00 hrs.

◆
AYUNTAMIENTO
Plaza de San Francisco
The old city hall may be under renovation when you see it. Diego de Riaño, a specialist in the richly ornate Plateresque style, started work on the building in 1527. The most striking example of his speciality is on the façade in Plaza de San Francisco. Inside, the style is mixed Gothic and baroque. Access is restricted.

The Ayuntamiento shows the Plateresque style at its best

◆
BASILICA DE LA MACARENA
Calle Bécquer
Built between 1941 and 1949 in baroque style, this was declared a 'minor basilica' by Pope Pius XII. It is distinguished for being the temple of what is probably the city's most loved and revered image of the Virgin. She is a baroque sculpture by an unknown artist, and her sad face is hauntingly marked by a teardrop. María Santísima de la Esperanza Macarena has received from her admirers a great wealth of gifts, which are

on display in the museum.
Open: (basilica) Tuesday to
Saturday 08.00–13.00 and
17.00–21.00 hrs; (museum)
Tuesday to Saturday 09.30–12.30
and 17.30–19.30 hrs.

◆◆
CAJA SAN FERNANDO
Plaza de San Francisco
The handsome central patio of
this imposing building is often
the setting for interesting
exhibitions. This savings bank
also has other exhibition centres:
Sala Imagen, corner of Calle
Imagen and Plaza de la
Encarnación; and **Sala Oriente**,
Calle Luis Montoto 112.
Open: check in local press.

◆◆◆
LA CARTUJA
Isla de la Cartuja
In 1400 the Bishop of Seville
founded the Carthusian
monastery of Santa María de las
Cuevas on the 'island', which is
actually a peninsula in the Río
Guadalquivir. The complex
developed in a mix of Gothic-
Mudéjar, Renaissance and
baroque styles, but it was
repeatedly damaged by flooding
and by earthquakes (1595 and
1755), which forced the monks to
abandon the site. La Cartuja was
fortified during the Spanish War
of Independence when it was
the southern headquarters of
Napoleon's army (1810 to 1812);
then in 1835 it was expropriated
by a short-lived Liberal
government, and an Englishman,
Charles Pickman, leased the
property to start a ceramics
factory. Production began in
1841 and only ceased in 1982.
Centuries earlier, the Moorish
Almohades, who arrived in the
12th century and made Seville
their capital, had dug caves here
to extract clay from which to
make their ceramics.
Pickman and Company adapted
the monastery buildings and
added others, including big kilns
with high chimneys. In 1964 La
Cartuja was declared a national
monument, and is now the
property of the Junta de
Andalucía.
A team with a budget of 5,000
million pesetas is restoring some
parts and converting others, with
a view first to pavilions and
exhibitions for Expo'92, and in
the long term to La Cartuja's new
role as the headquarters of the
Andalucian Institute for the

WHAT TO SEE

Conservation of the Cultural Heritage. There will be a museum, and the plan is that the public should be able to see restoration work whilst it is in progress.

◆
CASA DE LA CONDESA DE LEBRIJA
Calle de la Cuna 18
There is restricted public access to the Countess of Lebrija's town house, which behind its somewhat forbidding façade is a typical Sevillan mansion. It is centred on a patio adorned with Mudéjar plasterwork and tiled friezes. What makes it exceptional is that it includes a wealth of Roman mosaics and other pieces gleaned from sites around the city, before they were protected for posterity. The most impressive mosaic was found in Itálica in 1914.
Open: by prior appointment, tel: 422 7802.

◆
CASA DE MONEDA
Calle Santander
Sadly dilapidated, this complex is due for extensive rebuilding, which will give the city another attractive and historic precinct. It was first a palace of the Almohade sultan Abbu Hafs, and after the Christian Reconquest it became a prison for notables. In the 16th century it became the place where precious metals from the colonies were turned into coins, and it served this purpose until the 18th century, when it was privatised and taken over by *los indianos*, wealthy people returned from the Americas, whose names are reflected in surrounding streets.

◆◆◆
CASA DE PILATOS
Plaza de Pilatos
Construction was started in 1480. The Marquis of Tarifa, Don Fabrique Enríquez de Ribera, returned from the Holy Land in 1521 and, so one story goes, modelled his town mansion on what he had deduced from the ruins of Pilate's house in Jerusalem. Now owned by the Duke of Medinaceli, it is regarded as the grandest private residence in Seville, with pleasingly blended Mudéjar and Renaissance styles. Much of it is open to the public. The best parts are the arcaded and galleried principal patio, with its gorgeous decorative ceramic tiles (*azulejos*) and delicate plasterwork, and the magnificent main staircase below a large cupola.

A collection of classical statuary is on display in the patio and surrounding rooms, and fine frescos have been uncovered in the Salón de los Frescos. The chapel has more fine Mudéjar and Plateresque plasterwork; and Francisco Pachego, father-in-law of Velázquez, was responsible for the ceiling paintings in the *salón* which bears his name.

Other rooms, their furnishings, decoration and exhibits give an insight into the lifestyle of an aristocratic family over the centuries.
Open: Monday to Friday 10.00–18.00 hrs; Saturday 10.00–13.00 hrs.

Delicate decoration and spacious grandeur at the Casa de Pilatos

WHAT TO SEE

◆◆◆
CATEDRAL
Plaza del Triunfo

In 1401 the Cathedral Chapter declared, 'Let us build a cathedral so huge that on seeing it people will think us madmen.' The site chosen was occupied by Seville's main mosque, which in turn stood on the site of a

The cathedral is a Gothic giant

Visigothic church. Work started and continued until 1506. Although the main structure of the Catedral de Santa María de la Sede is Gothic, some embellishments and additions are late Gothic, Plateresque and baroque. It is a place of superlatives: the third largest Christian church in the world after Saint Peter's in Rome and Saint Paul's in London; the largest Gothic cathedral; the largest interior space of all with a width of some 272 feet (83m), a length of 313 feet (95m) and a height of 98 feet (30m). To that may be added: probably the most gloomy and probably the most richly endowed with art in all forms. Surrounding buildings prevent a view of the cathedral's huge bulk and its flying buttresses, but they can be appreciated by looking down from the **Giralda** (see separate entry). Inside, Gothic columns rising to the vaulted ceiling create five naves, but here too it is difficult to get a complete impression of the huge size because the view is restricted by the *coro* (choir) and **Capilla Mayor** (high altar). This is one of the cathedral's showpieces, with Christ's life depicted in 36 tableaux on gilded hardwood. Measuring 59 feet (18m) wide and 65 feet (20m) high, this altarpiece is the biggest in Christendom and was completed between 1482 and 1564. The **Coro** is screened by similar wrought-iron grilles to those of the Capilla Mayor, and the carving of its ebony wood stalls in Mudéjar-Renaissance style was completed in 1478. The **Capilla Real** (Royal Chapel) was completed in 1575, with mainly Plateresque decoration. The tombs of Alfonso X, *el Sabio* (The Wise), and his mother are on either side of the entrance. In the centre of the nave an elaborately worked silver urn contains the supposedly uncorrupted remains of Fernando III, *el Santo*. A 13th-century carving of larch wood depicts *La Virgen de los Reyes*, patron of Seville, to whom the 17th-century altar is dedicated. The tombs of Pedro I, *el Cruel*, and Pilar de Padilla are in the chapel's crypt. There are more chapels, which seen all together might provide an overdose of repetitive religiosity, but which viewed singly display work of great artistic merit.

A wealth of gold and silverware is on display in the **Sacristia Mayor**. Paintings in the **Sacristia de los Calices** include works by Martínez Montañes, Valdés Leál, Zurbarán and Goya. The **Sala Capitular** is an elliptical room designed for meetings of the Cathedral Chapter. Murillo painted the Immaculate Conception in the dome and there is also a series of eight other works by him. Cristóbal Colón's body spent a brief time in the cathedral after it was brought from Cuba. His monument, known as **Columbus' Tomb**, has figures representing Spain's four kingdoms of the time. Outside, the **Patio de los Naranjos**, which was the *sahn* (ablution courtyard) of the original mosque, has many orange trees (*naranjos*). See also **La Giralda** below.

Open: Monday to Saturday 11.00–17.00 hrs; Sunday 14.00–18.00 hrs.

'Columbus' Tomb'

WHAT TO SEE

◆
CONVENTO DE SAN LEANDRO
Plaza San Leandro
The nuns do a good trade in their *yemas de San Leandro*, which are sweets made from egg yolks. The church has an impressive altarpiece by Martínez Montañes.

◆◆
CONVENTO DE SANTA CLARA
Calle Santa Clara
Gothic and Mudéjar elements are blended in the convent, which is approached through a peaceful, tree-filled patio. Above it rises the 13th-century Torre de Don Fabrique, built in the transitional style from Romanesque to Gothic. The small collection of the Museo Arqueológico Municipal is on display in the tower.
Open: (museum) 09.00–17.00 hrs.

◆
CONVENTO DE SANTA INES
Calle Doña María Coronel
María Coronel used hot oil to disfigure her face so as to shake off the besotted Pedro I, *el Cruel*, and then took refuge in this Gothic-Mudéjar convent where her body lies. At the revolving door, nuns sell images of her as well as sweets which they make.

◆◆
CONVENTO DE SANTA PAULA
Calle Santa Paula 11
Here the nuns sell sweets made from Seville's bitter oranges as well as jams and marmalades. Gothic, Mudéjar and Renaissance styles coexist harmoniously. Notable features are the main portico and the cloister. There is also a small museum.

◆◆◆
EXPO'92 UNIVERSAL EXHIBITION
Isla de la Cartuja
It is impossible to avoid using superlatives in a description of the greatest ever Universal Exhibition, from 20 April to 12 October 1992. It is equally impossible to detail all that there will be to see and enjoy—to learn about the past, present and future, to be inspired, to be thrilled and to be entertained by the greatest performers, directors and technicians in all forms of expression. To state it as simply as possible: this is an enormous 'show off' event by 110 nations and Spain's 17 autonomous regions, of the history, culture, technology and prospects of some 80 per cent of humanity; by international organisations like Unicef and the Red Cross; by Spanish and multinational corporations. The programme includes over 50,000 live performances in 21 venues on the site and in the city. There will be sports events, horse shows, bullfights, gala parades, street performers . . . the list goes on. After a filling of culture and learning, relaxation and leisure can be taken at terraces, bars, restaurants and discos. When the pavilions close at 22.00 hrs, Expo-Night opens with a multimedia show over the lake, featuring fountains, lights, lasers, music and sometimes fireworks. The Palenque becomes a huge dance floor, offering a variety of music. This is the world's biggest, most action-packed party, going on until 04.00 hrs each day. The exhibition's theme, 'The Age of Discovery',

although commemorating the
quincentenary of Cristóbal
Colón's first voyage to the New
World, celebrates all of human
discovery and looks to the future.
A fascinating array of traditional,
modern and futuristic buildings,
designed by many of the world's
leading architects, has arisen on
Expo'92's 530-acre (215-hectare)
site. Water in cascades and
fountains and other forms
features in many of the pavilions.
Some half a million trees and
plants of almost 400 different
species, many from the
Americas, and 22 miles (35 km)
of hedges have been planted,
which, together with water
cooling and moisturising systems
have been planned to create a
microclimate on the site, with the
temperature several degrees
lower than elsewhere in Seville.
Some 20 million people are
expected to visit Expo'92 and
about half of them will be
foreigners. It is suggested that 10
days will be needed to see the
whole exhibition properly. A lot
of planning has gone into
ensuring easy access to the site,
as well as the visitor's comfort
and enjoyment once there.

◆◆◆
EXPO SITE
Isla de la Cartuja
Expo'92 was prepared with the
long-term view of opening up
museums, exhibition centres and
gardens on the site, and some
special attractions such as the
Planetarium. For the latest
details, consult tourist offices;
and see also the information on
venues under **Culture,
Entertainment and Nightlife**.

*La Cartuja's old monastery was
chosen as the hub of Expo'92—
the world's biggest party*

◆
FUNDACIÓN LUIS CERNUDA
Calle Harinas 5
The Diputación de Sevilla
(Provincial Council) sponsors
cultural events and exhibitions at
this venue.
Open: usually Tuesday to
Saturday 11.00–14.00 and
18.00–21.00 hrs.

WHAT TO SEE

◆◆◆
GIRALDA
Plaza del Triunfo
The Almohades began the
building of their main mosque in
1172. In 1184 their emir, Abu
Yacub Yusuf, ordered that it
should have a minaret which
would surpass in beauty that of
any other mosque. Now known
as the Giralda, it has become the
bell tower of the cathedral and
the emblem of a Christian city.
Its brick walls carry graceful
sebka decoration, and rise from
a square base on foundations
which include Roman tablets. In
1198 four superimposed bronze
spheres were placed as the
minaret's crowning ornament,
but they were destroyed by an
earthquake in the 14th century.
Despite this (and later
additions), the Giralda remains
a classic illustration of the
Almohades' skill at achieving
grandeur through simplicity.
In 1558 work started on adding
the present belfry and upper
tower in the prevailing
Renaissance style. Some 330 feet
(100m) above ground, it was
topped by a bronze *giraldilla*
(weathervane) in the form of a
figure of Faith. A ramp inside the
tower, which horsemen could
use, leads to the top from which
there are splendid views of the
cathedral, La Cartuja and the
spreading city. It is a deafening
experience to be in the tower
when the belfry's 24 bells are
being rung.
Open: Monday to Saturday
11.00–17.00 hrs; Sunday
14.00–18.00 hrs.

**The Giralda, built to be the
world's most beautiful minaret**

◆◆◆
HOSPITAL DE LA CARIDAD
Temprado
At the age of 34, Miguel de
Mañara, who had been a rich
man about town, turned to a life
of religious observance and
good works. His wife's

Hospital de la Caridad

unexpected death is thought to
have been the motivation. The
view has long been held that
Tirso de Molina's Don Juan
character, who first appears in
his play *Condenado por
Desconfiado*, was based on
Mañara; but the play was written
when Mañara was still a child.
One of the reformed man's first
acts was to join a religious
society which cared for the poor.
He became its leader and
transformed it into the Very
Humble Brotherhood. The
Hospital de la Caridad (Charity)

WHAT TO SEE

was where they cared for their charges. Today, it serves as a home for old people. The interest for visitors is in the chapel, built between 1645 and 1721. Valdés Leál painted the frescos in the presbytery cupola, and two famous death paintings which dramatically show life's transitory nature: Christ holds a scale inscribed *in ictu oculi*, in the blink of an eye. The chapel also has a number of works in different styles by Murillo; and Pedro Roldén painted the *Holy Burial* which is the main feature of the altarpiece. Mañara is buried in the crypt.
Open: 10.00–13.00 and 16.00–19.00 hrs.

◆
HOSPITAL DE CINCO LLAGAS
Andueza
The new Andalucian Parliament building is one of the city's biggest and finest examples of Renaissance civil architecture. Its debating chamber will be in the church, designed in 1558 by Hernáan Ruiz, who also designed the additions to the Giralda. The name means 'Hospital of the Five Wounds'. Founded in 1545, it was a private hospital until 1837, and then a public hospital until the mid 1960s.

◆◆
HOSPITAL DE LOS VENERABLES
Plaza Venerables
Los Venerables were the retired priests for whom this home was completed in 1687. It is one of Seville's many fine baroque buildings, and is also significant for having works by both Valdés

Leál and his son Lucas Valdés. The father did the ceiling frescos, and his son did those on the walls. There are also works by Herrera the Elder, Pedro Roldán, Alonso Cano and Martínez Montañes.
Open: Monday to Saturday 10.00–14.00 and 16.00–20.00 hrs; Sunday 10.00–14.00 hrs.

◆
HOTEL ALFONSO XIII
Calle San Fernando 2
The king of the same name opened this luxurious hotel in time for the Ibero-América exhibition. His grandson the present king Don Juan Carlos, reopened it after an extensive renovation towards the end of the 1970s. It follows the traditional Sevillan style of a house built round a patio, but on an enlarged scale. Taking an elegant, expensive tea is one way of viewing the interior, the guests and old-fashioned staff.

◆◆
IGLESIA JESÚS DEL GRAN PODER Y IGLESIA SAN LORENZO
Plaza San Lorenzo
The Mudéjar church of San Lorenzo has been much remodelled but it retains notable pieces of religious art from the 13th to 18th centuries, including a main altarpiece by Martínez Montañes, and another in the Capilla de la Concepción by Francisco Pachego. The adjoining modern, baroque-style church of Jesús el Poder (Jesus the Powerful) has an image of Christ (by Juan de Mesa in 1620), whose heel is kissed to speed the answering of prayers. The

One of the city's many images, at the Iglesia del Gran Poder

cofradía (brotherhood) of this image is one the city's most prominent, and its *paso* (float) for carrying the image in procession is one of the most elaborate. It can be seen in the museum together with the rest of the rich treasure 'owned' by the image. *Open:* (museum) 08.30–13.30 and 18.00–21.00 hrs.

◆◆
IGLESIA DE LA MAGDALENA
Plaza Magdalena
This big church has recently received the attention of renovators. It was built in 1609 on the site of an earlier church which had collapsed, and is notable for its polychrome cupolas and belfries. The interior, with three aisles, big transept and numerous chapels,

is very heavily decorated with frescos, paintings, plasterwork and polychrome reliefs. There are works by Valdés Leál, Lucas Valdés, Pedro Roldán, Juan Bautista Vazquez, Francisco Pachego and Zurbarán among others.

◆◆
IGLESIA DE SAN SALVADOR
Plaza Salvador
What is popularly regarded as the city's second cathedral was begun in 1674 on the site of a mosque, whose patio still exists. The church is most admired for its baroque altarpiece, and for the much venerated image of *Jesús de la Pasión* (Jesus of the Passion), carved by Martínez Montañes. It also has Juan de Mesa's carving of *Cristo del Amor* (Christ of Love). *Open:* 08.00–10.30 and 18.30–21.00 hrs.

WHAT TO SEE

Iglesia de Santa Ana

◆
IGLESIA DE SANTA ANA
Calle Pelay Correa
First built in the 13th century and rebuilt, remodelled and renovated through subsequent centuries, this church is unusual in Seville because of its brick construction, in a transitional style between Romanesque and Gothic. Inside, it boasts a fine altarpiece and a central choir.

◆
LA MAESTRANZA (PLAZA DE TOROS)
Paseo de Cristóbal Colón
Seville's bullring was completed in the 1760s and can seat 14,000 spectators. From April to October there are bullfights every Sunday evening. Guided tours are available on other days.

◆
MONOLITOS ROMANOS
Calle Marmoles
Three columns, 3 feet (1 m) in diameter and 29 feet (9 m) high, remain from what is believed to have been a Roman temple to Hercules. The two columns in Alameda de Hércules were taken from this site.

◆
MURALLAS
Ronda de Capuchinos
Between the Puerta de Córdoba and Puerta de Macarena is a stretch of city walls (*murallas*) with a number of turrets and towers dating from the Moorish fortifications around the city, though changed and restored. Adjoining the Puerta de Córdoba is the Capella de San Hermenegildo, built where legend says the Visigothic prince was martyred.

◆◆◆
MUSEO ARQUEOLÓGICO
Plaza de América, Parque de María Luisa
The Archaeological Museum occupies two floors of the Renaissance palace built for the 1929 Ibero-América Exhibition, and is highly regarded by professionals. Most of the pieces on display were found in the vicinity, and range from the Paleolithic period to the time when Mudéjar craftsmen were at work. The strongest part of the collection is of Roman material, which includes notable statues and busts of Alexander the Great, Venus, Diana and Mercury. A sculpture of the Emperor Hadrian, who was born in Itálica, stands before a big mosaic from the 2nd century, and the serenely composed Head of Hispania holds one's attention. For many the museum's greatest prize is the Carambolo Treasure, discovered in a hillside very close to the city in 1958. It comprises 21 pieces of finely worked 24-carat gold jewellery, which was probably buried with a king or priest of Tartessos in the 8th century BC. The Phoenician inscriptions on the base are the oldest so far discovered in Spain.
Open: Tuesday to Saturday 10.00–14.00hrs.

◆
MUSEO DE ARTE CONTEMPORANEO
Santo Tomás 5
The Modern Art Museum is housed in the Cilla del Cabildo Catedral (Cathedral Tax House), which was built in 1770 and in some ways resembles the nearby Lonja. The museum has a policy of promoting young and rising Andalucian artists in painting, sculpture, ceramics and tapestry. Prominent local artists of the present day who are represented include Gordillo, Saénz, Pérez Aguilera, Francisco Molina and Blanca Mencos. There are also works by internationally well-known names like Chillida, Manrique, Miró, Tàpies and Saura. Changing exhibitions featuring an artist or a theme are held regularly.
Open: Tuesday to Friday 10.00–14.00 and 17.00–20.00hrs; Saturday and Sunday 10.00–14.00hrs.

◆◆
MUSEO DE ARTES Y COSTUMBRES POPULARES
Plaza de América, Parque de María Luisa
The Mudéjar Pavilion built for the 1929 Ibero-América Exhibition is home to this fascinating museum. In contrast to the archaeological museum opposite, it gives an insight into local life of more recent times. Traditional work methods and crafts are celebrated in re-creations of rooms and workshops, and there are displays of crafts for which the city and area are best known: lace, weaving, silver and gold work, and pottery. Dress and accessories for court life, everyday wear and religious festivals are also shown, as are furniture, domestic ornaments and musical instruments.
Open: Tuesday to Saturday 10.00–14.00hrs.

WHAT TO SEE

MUSEO DE BELLAS ARTES
Plaza del Museo
After the Prado in Madrid, this is Spain's most important collection of fine art. The museum was opened in 1835 in the large baroque Convento de la Merced, which has recently undergone extensive renovations and improvements. Much of the collection came from convents in Seville, and besides paintings there are sculptures, goldwork, embroidery, furniture and pottery. The earliest works are Gothic religious panels and imagery from the 13th to 15th centuries; the best-represented painters are Zurbarán, Murillo and Valdés Leál. Francisco Zurbarán (1598–1664) came from Extremadura and lived in Seville from 1629 to 1658. His *Apotheosis of Saint Thomas Aquinas* is regarded as the finest canvas in the museum. Bartolomé Murillo (1617–92) is represented by numerous works, among which the *Virgen de Servilleta, San Tomas de Villanueva* and *Santas Justa and Rufina* are some of the possessions the museum is most proud of. Valdés Leál (1622–90) was a founder member of the Seville Arts Academy in 1660. His grand canvases are filled with vitality, in contrast with the macabre pessimism of his two works in the church of the Hospital de la Caridad (see separate entry). Also represented are artists of the '1560 Generation'—Pachego, Varela, Roelas, Alonso Cano and Velázquez—and El Greco.
Open: Tuesday to Saturday 10.00–14.00 and 16.00–19.00 hrs.

MUSEO-CASA DE MURILLO
Santa Teresa
Bartolomé Esteban Murillo was born in Seville in 1617, and his life virtually spanned the period now known as the Golden Age of Spanish art. He died in 1692 in the Convento de Santa Teresa, opposite what is now the museum. It is one of numerous houses in the Barrio de Santa Cruz where he is believed to have lived. The restored house was opened in 1982, and has a bedroom and studio-workshop set up as they may have looked in Murillo's time. There are also displays of furniture and domestic utensils, and paintings. The house has a typical Sevillan patio.
Open: Tuesday to Friday 10.00–14.00 and 16.00–19.00 hrs; Saturday and Sunday 10.00–14.00 hrs.

MUSEO NÁUTICO
Paseo de Cristóbal Colón
Housed in the Torre del Oro, the nautical museum has a small collection of drawings, etchings, maps, historical documents and navigation instruments, giving an outline of Seville's naval history.
Open: Tuesday to Saturday 10.00–14.00 hrs; Sunday 10.00–13.00 hrs.

PABELLÓN MUDÉJAR
Plaza de América, Parque María Luisa
This is the building which houses the Museo de Artes Populares, in addition to which it has various interesting exhibitions.

◆
PALACIO DE LAS DUEÑAS
Dueñas
This is the Sevillan residence of
the Duke and Duchess of Alba,
who permit limited public
access. It has an arched and
galleried patio-garden
decorated with delicate Mudéjar
plasterwork and filled with
palms and fruit trees. More fine
plasterwork and tiles are used in
the interior decoration, and the
rooms are filled with the
treasures acquired by
generations of one of Spain's
leading aristocratic families.
Open: by prior appointment
(tel: 422 0956).

◆
PALACIO DE SAN TELMO
Avenida de Roma
Now the headquarters of the
Junta de Andalucía, the palace
was completed in the early 18th
century to serve as a maritime
college, and is named after San
Telmo, the patron saint of
navigators. The saint's statue is
featured on the main portal,
flanked by figures of San
Hermenegildo, the Visigothic
martyr, and San Fernando, who
took Seville from the Arabs.
Prominent Sevillanos are
depicted in 19th-century statues
which top the northern façade.

◆◆◆
PARQUE DE MARÍA LUISA
*Avenida de María Luisa, Paseo
de las Delicias, Avenida de
Isabel la Católica*
The park consists of half of the
gardens of the Palacio de San
Telmo. It takes its name from
María Luisa Fernanda, sister of
Queen Isabel II and duchess of
the Montpensier family, who

Parque de María Luisa

donated the gardens to the city
in 1893. The park is a green and
shady refuge in a city where the
air can hang very hot and still
during the summer. It has areas
of carefully tended formal
gardens, trellises and ponds,
other areas of bowers and
grottos, and parts where a
profusion of exotic trees flourish
amid untamed undergrowth.
Among the statues are those of
Princess María Luisa, the
Romantic poet Gustavio Béquer,
the Quintero playwright brothers
and the Machado poet brothers.
For the 1929 Ibero-América
Exhibition, pavilions and other
buildings were constructed on
the park's periphery and around
the Plaza de América.

◆◆
PLAZA DE ESPAÑA

Avenida de Isabel la Católica
Aníbal González was the principal architect for the 1929 Ibero-América Exhibition, and this was its largest construction. It consists of an arcaded brick-faced building in a semi-circle around a big plaza which has a tall fountain at its centre and is usually packed with friendly and hungry doves. A boating pond follows the line of the building and is spanned by small bridges decorated with ceramic tiles, including a series depicting identifying features of each of Spain's 50 provinces. The buildings, which are not open to the general public, are used as government offices, including that of the Civil Governor for Seville province.

Not just a splendid civic building, Plaza de España is also popular for its boating lake and doves

◆◆◆
REALES ALCÁZARES
Plaza del Triunfo
After their capture of Seville in 712, Moorish military chiefs built a fortress on this site. In the 9th century the fortress was transformed into a palace for the emir, Abderraman II. Part of its surrounding wall running from the Barrio de Santa Cruz to the Plaza del Triunfo still exists. During the 11th century the palace was further enlarged by

In the Jardines del Alcázar

the Almohades, who made Seville their capital, built the new great mosque and Giralda, and set about adding new buildings and gardens to the Alcázar. Remaining examples of their embellishments are the **Patio del Yeso** (Plasterwork Court) and **Patio del Crucero** (Transept). Later the Christian

Castilian kings brought their northern architectural styles to the palace: Alfonso X added three large Gothic halls; Alfonso XI's contribution was the **Sala de Justicia** with its fine plasterwork and Mudéjar panelling, which is the oldest to be seen in the city. Pedro I, *el Cruel*, did at least one good deed when he ordered the building of the Mudéjar palace which remains as the core of the Reales Alcázares today and is widely considered as the richest gem of Mudéjar secular architecture. He called for craftspeople and artists from Granada and Toledo, and incorporated fragments collected from earlier Moorish buildings, particularly from Medina Azahara in Córdoba. The inspiration of the style of Medina Azahara is very evident in the **Salón de Embajadores** (Ambassadors' Hall), where columns support triple horseshoe arches to form the doorways along three of its walls. The wooden cupola of this exceptional hall is a 15th-century addition by Diego Ruiz. Arabic characters above the entrance arch repeat the words 'only God conquers'. It is in this hall that the public and private sections of the palace join. The former is centred on the galleried **Patio de las Doncellas** (Maidens) with its fine frieze and foliated arches. Domestic quarters surround the more hidden **Patio de las Muñecas** (Dolls), where delicate columns and capitals, almost certainly from Medina Azahara, support the galleries. Successive monarchs made additions to Rey Don Pedro's palace, most notably a Gothic

Mudéjar brilliance at the Reales Alcázares

church built by Fernando and Isabela, and a set of apartments built by Carlos V. The latter was also responsible for extending the **Jardines del Alcázar**, where previously the feared Pedro had done some of his misdeeds, and where Doña María de Padilla took her bath and titillated watching courtiers. Today, these rambling gardens are just the place to seek relief from the sun and city hubbub. The **Pabellón de Carlos V** is an attractive addition to the orchard; and Spain's first Bourbon king, Felipe V, added the **Apeadero** where exhibitions are held.
Open: Monday to Friday 09.00–12.45 and 15.00–17.00 hrs; Sunday 09.00–12.45 hrs.

WHAT TO SEE

The Torre del Oro was once part of the city's defences

◆
SALA VILLASÍS
Pasaje Villasís 6
This is the exhibition centre of the Caja El Monte savings bank. It is usually worthwhile to check what is being shown.
Open: usually Tuesday to Saturday 11.00–14.00 and 18.00–21.00 hrs.

◆
TORRE DE LA PLATA
Calle Santander
The Tower of Silver was finished by the Almohades in 1221 as part

of the defensive wall which ran from their Alcázar to the Torre del Oro. Later it fell into disrepair and became hidden and largely unknown, even by Sevillans. After its current restoration, it will stand proud with the Giralda and Torre del Oro as the third of Seville's medieval towers. See also **Casa de Moneda**, which is here.

◆◆◆
TORRE DEL ORO
Paseo de Cristóbal Colón
After the Giralda, the 'Tower of Gold' is the second most distinctive tower in the cityscape, and it enjoys a prominent position on the riverbank. The Almohades completed it, together with a long-gone tower on the opposite bank, in 1220. A chain stretching across the river between the two was part of the city's defensive system. Golden tiles on the original roof gave the tower its name. The rounded top section was added in 1760. See also **Museo Náutico**.

◆◆
UNIVERSIDAD (FABRICA DE TABACO)
Calle San Fernando
The science and law faculties of Seville University now occupy the second largest building in Spain, which was built as a tobacco factory and completed in 1771. The buildings are arranged around two large courtyards. It was here that the mythical Carmen of the opera worked with more than 5,000 other women rolling cigarettes, a sight considered too sexually provocative for most men to witness.

Walks in Seville

There is no better way to get the feel of a city than to walk its streets and alleys. The outlines of two daytime walks are suggested here. Without allowing for time spent visiting places of interest or for shopping and refreshments, each of the walks will take less than two hours at a gentle pace. Places shown in **bold** type are more fully described in the preceding individual entries. Both walks start and end in the Plaza del Triunfo.

◆◆◆
WALK 1: CENTRO

The Plaza del Triunfo is the epicentre of the city's sightseeing attractions, as it is surrounded by the **Catedral, Reales Alcázares, Archivo de Indias** and the Casa de la Diputación de Sevilla (Antiguo Hospital del Rey) which has an exhibition centre. In the centre of the plaza is La Inmaculada, a monument to the Immaculate Conception, much venerated in the city. The Triunfo memorial recalls a big earthquake of 1755. Leave on the right side of the cathedral, to reach the very attractive Plaza de Virgen de los Reyes, where the tables of the Meson El Giradillo spill into the street and horse carriages continuously pass by the elaborate central lamppost. On the left, behind orange trees, is the Convento de la Encarnación, whose oldest parts date from the 14th century. Opposite is the coloured front of the Palacio Arzobispal, dating from the 16th century, which is occupied by the Cardinal of Seville. Abutting the cathedral rises the magnificent **Giralda**. Below it on the right, a doorway with a grill gives sight of the Cathedral's Patio de los Naranjos. Walk beside it along Calle Alemanes, passing the steps of 'las Gadas', known since the time when Cervantes was in the city as a loitering place of rascals. You pass an impressive archway, another grilled entrance to the patio, and horse carriages sheltering in the shade of orange trees. On the other side of the street are some touristy eateries and a good bookshop for travel guides and maps. Turn right up Avenida de la Constitución and enter Plaza de San Francisco to note the intricate Plateresque façade of the **Ayuntamiento**, which, after its renovation, will no longer be used as a working city hall. A few interesting shops line the opposite side of the plaza. If shopping is your main interest, you may now want to go up Calle Cuna and lose yourself in the maze of streets, including Calle Sierpes, which stretch to the left and make up the principal shopping area. To continue with the walk, enter pedestrianised Calle Cuna, at the top left of Plaza Salvador, and (after some windowshopping) go left into Calle Campana. On the corner with Calle Sierpes, Confiteria la Campana is the ideal place for coffee and something sweet to eat, or for cooling, creamy and delicious *helados* (ice creams). Bearing right you pass Plaza Duque de la Victoria and the El Cortes Inglés department store to enter Calle Alfonso XII. Soon you reach the tree-filled Plaza del Museo in front of the **Museo**

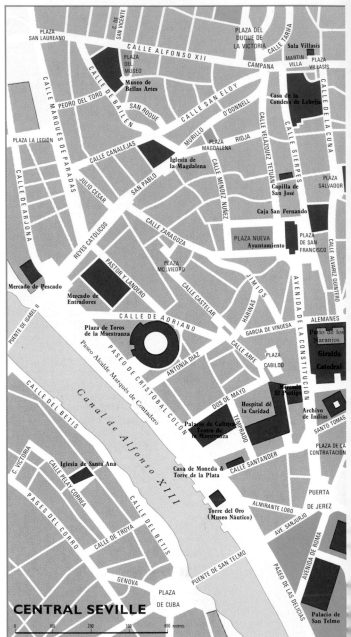

CENTRAL SEVILLE

0   100   200   300   400 metres

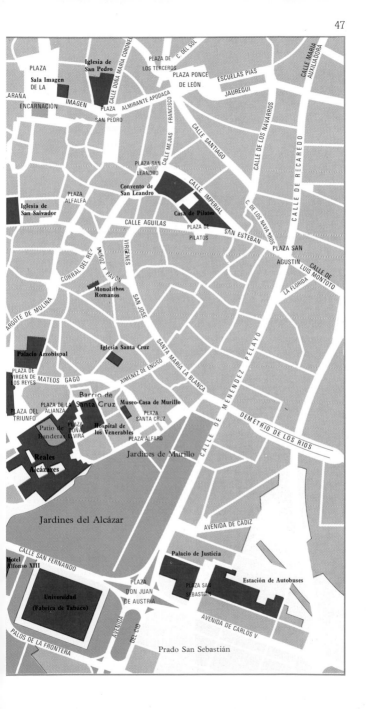

de Bellas Artes. Leave on the left far side of the plaza to enter Calle San Rouque, cross right into Calle Bailén and right into Calle San Pablo with the **Iglesia de la Magdalena** on your right. Galerías Preciados department store is opposite. Cross at the pedestrian crossing and continue right into Calle Reyes Católicos. When you reach Paseo de Cristóbal Colón, go left and cross at the first pedestrian crossing, then go left along the riverside. The bridge to the right, Puente Isabel II, brings traffic from the Triana district. You have a view of some

La Maestranza bullring

colourful old buildings along Calle Betis on the west bank. Most likely there will be rowers on the river as well as some pleasure cruise craft. On the left is the white and ochre **La Maestranza** bullring. Next comes the imposing façade of the new Teatro de la Maestranza. The pleasant Paseo Marqués de Contadero continues to the **Torre del Oro** with its small **Museo Náutico**. At the open-air café bar here, you may want to take refreshments and rest awhile as you take in the scene. Cross the Paseo Colón and go into Calle Santander where you find the **Casa de Moneda** and **Torre de la Plata**, then go left into Calle Temprado for the **Hospital de la Caridad**. Continue into Calle Dos de Mayo and look out for the old advertisements in the ceramic tiles. Narrow streets on the left may tempt you to meander a while in the interesting quarter of El Arenal. Turn right along Calle Dos de Mayo, and ahead is the Mercado El Postigo crafts market. Close by through an archway on the left is the enclosed, recently renovated Plaza del Cabildo. Leave it the same way and go left into Avenida de la Constitución. Cross over and go right, with the Lonja on your left. On the corner with Calle Santo Tomás is the Torre de Ab-el-Agiz, a remaining part of the wall which united the Moorish Alcázar and Torre del Oro. Legend says the banner of Castile was hoisted here when Fernando III, *el Santo*, took the city in 1248. Left along Calle Santo Tomás brings you back to Plaza del Triunfo.

◆◆◆
WALK 2: BARRIO DE SANTA CRUZ

From the Plaza del Triunfo, on the left of the **Reales Alcázares**, go through the archway into the enclosed rectangle of Patio Banderas. From the far side, look back for a view of the **Giralda** and then leave by the covered passage on the left. The buzz of the city dies away as you enter the enclosed quarter of the old Judería, where Fernando III allowed Jews from Toledo and elsewhere to settle. (The Moorish Almohades had expelled the original Jewish community.) From now on, you are in a barrio whose charm does not change, no matter how many tourists pass over the cobbles of its narrow streets and small squares, lined by whitewashed buildings with ochre-coloured decoration, black wrought-iron *rejas* (grills) and balconies usually bright with flowers. Heavy doorways or solid grills hide private patios where more flowers bloom and fountains play. At times the air is heavy with the scent of orange blossom and jasmine. Progress through the barrio is likely to be delayed by sorties into art and crafts shops, or by lingering awhile at an outdoor café.

Linger in the Patio de Banderas

WALKS IN SEVILLE

From the covered passage, Calle Judería leads into Calle Vida and its small square, in which the Café Copenhague has tables and chairs. On the right and to the left is Callejon del Agua, lined by a wall separating the barrio from the gardens of the Reales Alcázares. The story goes that this alley got its name from the aqueduct which once ran along it. Shortly, turn into Calle Pimienta. A plaque recalls that number 14 was once the home of María Guerrero, the actress after whom the theatre in Madrid, where Spain's national drama company is based, was named. Go left into Calle Susona. Where it veers to the right, a ceramic tile with the painting of a skull recalls one of the barrio's legends. In the 15th century Jews led by one named Susón conspired to kill the most prominent Christians and seize control of the city. One of those on their list was the secret lover of Susón's daughter, Susona, who exposed the scheme to him. Her father was condemned to death and in time she was deserted by her lover. She died after a miserable life and left a will stating that, for her shame, her skull should be displayed above her doorway.

Plaza Doña Elvira is named after a luckier lady. She inherited the buildings around it from her father who had benefited from Enrique III's confiscation of Jewish property under the influence of the Inquisition. Go right into Calle Gloria and then into Plaza de los Venerables, which is dominated by the **Hospital de los Venerables**. Note the attractive entrance into Calle

Jamerdana before going into Calle Reinosa and right into Calle Lope de Rueda, both streets named after poets. In Plaza de Alfaro, which overlooks the Jardines de Murillo beyond the barrio, there is just the type of pretty balcony on which Rosina might stand in the opera *The Barber of Seville*. Next door is Plaza de Santa Cruz. A fine wrought-iron cross at its centre commemorates the church which once stood on this site, and which was destroyed by French forces in the Peninsular War. You might want to return here at night, when the plaza has a different look in the light of its lamps, and enjoy the elegance and good food of La Albahaca, followed by a flamenco *tablao* at Los Gallos. Leave the plaza by Calle Santa Teresa. It is named after the revered mystic from Avila who founded the Convento de San José in 1596. The nuns have some Teresian relics. You may be able to visit their church which, among its treasures, has a reproduction of the image of the Virgen de Guadalupe, patron saint of Mexico. Opposite is the **Museo-Casa de Murillo**. Turn left into Calle Ximenez and go ahead into Plaza de la Alianza, where you may want to sit at the outdoor tables of the café bar and take in the sight of the very pretty plaza, with the Giralda above the rooftops. From here you can return to the Plaza del Triunfo.

If you want to carry on walking, backtrack a bit and go left into Calle Rodrigo Caro to Calle Mateos Gago, a street of some shopping interest. Next right is Calle Meson del Moro, where in

1491 a Morisco was allowed to open an eating house in the city for the first time. The present Restaurante Meson del Moro has accurately restored a section of an old Jewish house. Go left into Calle Ximenez to reach Calle Santa María de la Blanca. Along this street there were once moneychangers' shops, the Jewish *azcuica* (market), and a synagogue. At the end, turn right towards the Jardines de Murillo and walk through or alongside the gardens. You pass a monument to Cristóbal Colón before reaching Calle San Fernando, lined on one side by student bars and eateries and on the other by the imposing bulk of the **Universidad**. Cross Calle San Fernando to go down Calle Doña María de Padilla, between the Universidad and **Hotel Alfonso XIII**. Turn right between it and the **Palacio de San Telmo**, and go round to see its impressive portal. Return along the other side of the Hotel Alfonso XIII, cross over San Fernando to go into the alley of San Gregorio, passing through the tiny Plaza de la Contratación to arrive back in Plaza del Triunfo.

Timeless Barrio de Santa Cruz

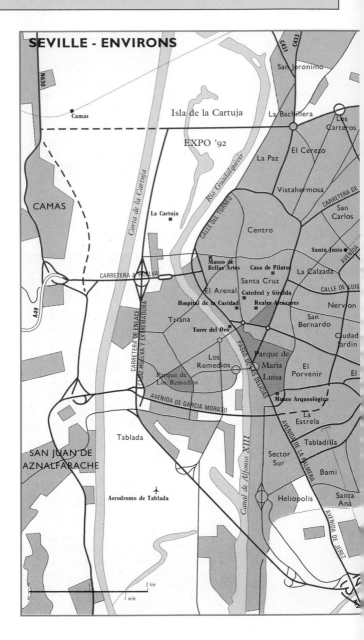

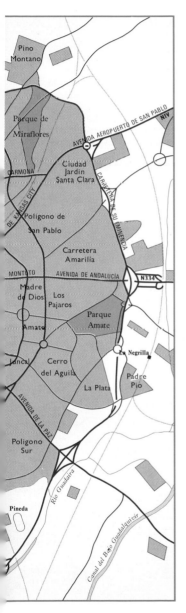

Excursions from Seville

Besides the great attraction of the city itself, Seville is a gateway to discovering more of Andalucía, Europe's most diversified region geographically and one of its most fascinating historically and culturally. If you are going to plan your own excursions, get a good map of the region, such as Firestone's, but make sure it is the latest and shows the new road network. It is a good idea to phone ahead to tourist offices to find out if anything special is going on and to enquire about availability of accommodation. Remember, generally places of interest are closed during the siesta (roughly 14.00–18.00 hrs), on Sunday afternoons and on Mondays.

Coach Tours

Advice and information about organised tours of different duration can be obtained from travel agents in Seville.

Al-Andalus Express

Vintage rolling stock has been beautifully restored in *belle époque* style to provide single and double compartments with showers, a luxury restaurant and bar coaches. Ask your travel agent, and make a booking well in advance if you want to be one of 80 passengers on this sumptuous train's gentle wanderings through Andalucía, on a route which takes in Córdoba and Granada, or another which goes to Jerez and the sherry lands. It is sheer indulgence at a high price, but will be an experience forever memorable.

EXCURSIONS FROM SEVILLE

◆
ALCALÁ DE GUADAIRA
6 miles (10 km) southeast
Now virtually a suburb of Seville, the town has spread out below the impressive castle built by the Almohades as an outer defence for their capital city. It is one of the best remaining examples of their military architecture. The town's San Miguel church was built as a mosque, and there are other Moorish remains.

◆◆◆
ANTEQUERA
102 miles (165 km) southeast
Prehistoric monuments show Antequera's strategic importance from earliest times. It was recognised by successive conquerors: Romans left their mark and so did the Moors. Prince Fernando captured it in 1410 and it became a forward base for the long assault on Granada. The town has a rich

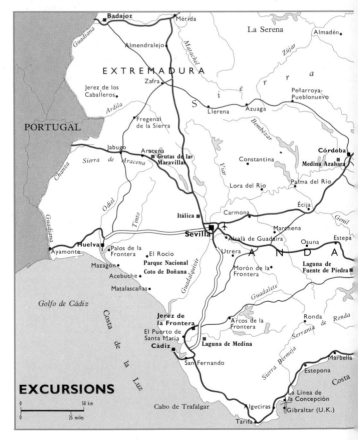

EXCURSIONS

legacy of churches, convents, monasteries and fine civil buildings in Renaissance, Mudéjar and baroque styles. Start by going up to the high ground on the town's southeastern edge. The **Alcazaba**, built by the Moors in the 14th century on the ruins of a Roman castle, features the fine **Torre del Papabellotas** belfry tower. Below the Alcazaba is the big church of **Santa María la**

White walls, blue sky—essence of Andalucia at Antequera

Mayor, completed in 1550 and recently restored, which has an impressive Plateresque façade and sparse interior graced by Mudéjar ceilings. It faces the **Arco de los Gigantes**, a Mannerist construction of 1585. To the east is **La Peña de los Enamorados** (Lovers' Rock). There is a legend that two lovers, a Muslim and a Christian, jumped from it to be together in death rather than apart in life. The **Museo Municipal**, in the 18th-century Palacio de Nájera, has one of the most beautiful bronze statues of Roman Spain yet discovered, *el Efebo*. Near by are the churches of **Encarnación**, 16th-century with notable Mudéjar coffered ceilings; and **San Sebastian**, 16th-century Renaissance style. The **Palacio Consistorial** (Town Hall) is a much-remodelled

Franciscan monastery, with a notable cloister. Adjoining it is **Los Remedios**, a 17th-century church dedicated to Antequera's patron saint. Among the many other fine churches, the most notable are the **Convento de San Zoilo** and **Iglesia del Carmen**. The **Conjunto Dolmenico**, just on the town's eastern edge, comprises two dolmens (tombs) of a people who lived in the area around 2000BC. The one known as **Menga** is the biggest and best-maintained of its type yet discovered anywhere. Built of 31 stone slabs hauled from elsewhere, some weighing 180 tons, it is 80 feet (25 m) deep and 12 feet (3.75 m) high. **Viera** is a smaller dolmen of similar construction.

Parque Natural Torcal de Antequera, 8 miles (13 km) south of the town, comprises 2,965 acres (1,200 hectares) of limestone formations shaped by wind and water into fantastic forms which visitors can view from marked paths. **Laguna de Fuente de Piedra**, 14 miles (23 km) northwest of the town off the Seville highway, is the only place in the peninsula where a large colony of pink flamingos regularly nests. Flocks of 15,000 pairs usually arrive in April and stay until early September. The lagoon is also home to other bird species, reptiles and amphibians.

Accommodation
The best place to stay is the **Parador Nacional**, García del Olmo (tel: (952) 84 00 61), 3-star, 55 rooms. It is a modern and spacious building in regional style.

Restaurants
The Parador is one of the best places to try local cooking. Another is **Chaplin**, Calle San Agustín 3 (tel: (952) 84 30 34).

ARACENA
56 miles (90 km) northwest
The **Grutas de las Maravillas** (Caves of Marvels) are the main draw for visitors to this town on the northern slopes of the Sierra de Aracena. Guided tours are taken deep into the caves, past large chambers and six lakes, to see brightly coloured rock forms. Times of tours should be checked with the tourist office. Other notable sights are the Iglesia de Nuestra Señora de la Asunción, with an impressive Renaissance façade, and, above the town, a church built by the Knights Templar in the 13th century which has a Mudéjar tower.

Most visitors go on to the small town of **Jabugo**, 11 miles (18 km) to the west. It has the highest reputation throughout Spain for its *pata negra* ham, so called because the brown breed of pigs from which it comes have black *patas* (feet). They roam the surrounding cork oak forests and live on a diet of acorns which gives a special flavour to their meat. Long curing takes place on the premises of local producers, which can be visited.

Restaurant
Casas, Calle Colmenitas 41, Aracenas (tel: (955) 11 00 44), is one of the best places to have lunch and enjoy the ham and pork for which the area is highly regarded.

◆◆
ARCOS DE LA FRONTERA

71 miles (115 km) south
Approached along the road from Jerez, Arcos presents a stunning sight, perched high on a cliffside above the Río Guadalete. Once in the town, follow signs to the Parador and make your way up the maze of twisting streets of the old quarter, with its mix of Moorish and Renaissance architecture. This is the way to the **Plaza de España**, from where there are wide views over the curving Guadalete and its plain. Facing the plaza is the façade of **Iglesia de Santa María**, originally Visigothic but mainly dating from the 16th to 18th centuries.

Accommodation
Parador Nacional Casa del Corregidor (tel: (956) 70 05 00), 44 rooms. One of Spain's many successful conversions of old buildings to make a comfortable hotel. It is also a good place for a meal.
Los Olivos, Calle San Miguel 3 (tel: (956) 70 08 11), is also comfortable, and is lower-priced.

Arcos de la Frontera is a clifftop maze of old streets

EXCURSIONS FROM SEVILLE

CÁDIZ
76 miles (123 km) southwest
Cádiz was founded by the
Phoenicians as 'Gadir' in 1100BC,
and has a just claim to be the
oldest continuously inhabited
city in the Western world. It
played an important maritime
role in Spain's conquest of the
New World, and from 1717 to
1778 held the monopoly of New
World trade. In 1797 the British
admiral Nelson bombarded the
city; during the Peninsular War it
was for a time the capital of
Spain; and in 1812 Spain's first
constitution was signed in the
Iglesia de San Felipe Neri.
Today the city of some 160,000
people is centred on a thin
promontory and its industrial
outskirts spread around a wide
bay, as do the fish farms of one of
its fastest growing industries. It
has a busy port and shipbuilding
yards. Tourist sights are limited:
the **Museo de Cádiz** displays
local archaeological finds and
has works by Murillo, Ribera and
Zurbarán as well as exhibits of
folkloric interest; the **Catedral**, in
Greco-Roman style, was started
in 1702 and took 136 years to
complete; in the **Oratorio de la
Santa Cueva** there are paintings
by Goya. It is in the maze of the
old quarter, behind fortified
entrance towers, that Cádiz
hides its charms and it is here
that the visitor will be inclined to
linger, perhaps to enjoy the wit
and freewheeling attitudes for
which the *gaditanos* are
renowned.
Castillo Santa Catalina looks out
across the Atlantic breakers.
High-rises back a good beach
but the province has better to

offer. A popular excursion is the
45-minute trip to Puerto de Santa
María on the *el Vapor* ferry
which departs from the port
entrance.

Restaurants
Fish is the favoured food, and
pescato frito is served
everywhere as a tapa. Two
restaurants to try: **El Faro**, Calle
San Felix 15 (tel: (956) 21 10 68),
is smart and pricey; **El
Sardinero**, Plaza de San Juan de
Dios 4 (tel: (956) 28 25 05), is
simple and moderately priced.

Special Events
Cádiz enjoys **Carnival**
(February/March) with great
abandon, making it one of the
liveliest and most colourful
celebrations in Europe.

CARMONA
20 miles (33 km) east
Every visitor to Seville should try
to visit this town, which has been
declared a National Monument.
You could even use it as a base,
as a more restful alternative to
Seville. It was a strategic site for
Paleolithic man, Iberians,
Carthaginians, Romans, who
built its walls, and Moors, who
fortified them. In the extensive
Necropolis Romana, which a
British archaeologist, George
Bonsor, excavated between 1881
and 1914, there are over 800
family tombs, some dated to the
1st century BC. The most
impressive are the Servilia,
almost the size of a villa, and the
Elefante, guarded by a statue of
an elephant. After the caliphate
in Córdoba collapsed, Carmona
was for a time the capital of a
taifa and its rulers raised fine

buildings. After its capture by Fernando III, *el Santo*, in 1247, it was favoured by successive monarchs and further endowed with fine architecture. Elements from both Moorish and later periods feature in the buildings along streets and squares, which follow the Roman town plan. The **Puerta de Sevilla**, main entry to the old town, is part of the Alcázar Bajo (Lower Fortress), built by the Romans and altered by the Moors. Close by, the tower of the 15th-century **Iglesia de San Pedro** was erected in 1704 and is a copy of the Giralda. Visitors can ask to see the patio of the **Ayuntamiento**, which is covered by a Roman mosaic depicting Medusa. **Plaza de San Fernando** is lined with buildings in which Mudéjar elements are prominent. The **Iglesia Santa María la Mayor** is a Gothic structure on the site of a mosque from which it retains the ablution patio and other elements. It has notable Plateresque altarpieces, ironwork and paintings. Two octagonal Roman towers flank the **Puerta de Córdoba**. The Moors' Alcázar Arriba (Upper Fortress) was converted into a palace by Pedro I, *el Cruel*, but was abandoned after an earthquake in the 16th century. It is now the very attractive Parador.

Accommodation

Casa de Carmona, 5-star, 30 rooms. Ultra-modern facilities, refined service and great elegance in 16th- and 17th-century buildings arranged around patios and interior gardens. The restaurant is only open to guests and their invitees.

Parador Nacional del Rey Don Pedro (tel: (95) 414 10 10), 4-star, 122 rooms. Waking up to look out across the extensive plain far below your bedroom window is a perfect start to the day. It is also a good place to eat.
Casa Carmelo, Calle San Pedro (tel: (95) 414 05 72), 1-star pension, 13 rooms. Around half the price of the Parador.

◆◆◆
CÓRDOBA

87 miles (140 km) northeast
Córdoba has had a glorious past. It was Rome's administrative city for its rich province of Baetica, and under the Muslim caliphacy it became Western Europe's biggest, most cultured city. Packed with monuments and echoes of the past, but in its own way living vibrantly in the present, this is a city which leaves an indelible mark in the memory. Most of Córdoba sits on the Río Guadalquivir's northern bank with sierras not far behind. It has a population of around 300,000 and is capital of a province whose variety and interest is being discovered by an increasing number of visitors. The city's greatest legacy is **La Mesquita**, the magnificent mosque which was begun in 785 and reached its present great size by 990. It ranks among the world's finest architectural treasures and its *mihrab* (prayer niche) is a special gem. After taking the city in 1236, Christians removed some of the mosque's 856 interior columns. During the 16th century they began building within it a Gothic **cathedral** which, as it took 243 years to complete, acquired

The 1,000-year-old Mesquita

decoration in later styles. The **Alcázar**, which was started in the 14th century as a palace of the Christian kings, has attractive water gardens and wide views from its towers. The **Puente Romano**, first restored by the Arabs and many times since, leads to the **Torre de la Calahorra**, a 14th-century guard tower where now a diorama and wax figures depict the life and history of Arabs, Jews and Christians in Córdoba and the rest of *Al-Andalus*. Downstream from the bridge are three Arab mills. In the oldest part, narrow streets are lined by some fine mansions and other buildings

whose wrought-iron gates lead to cool, beflowered patios where fountains play. Here is **La Judería** quarter, where the great Jewish scholar Maimónides was born and a synagogue of the 14th century has survived. Cervantes mentions the **Posada del Potro** (Inn of the Colt) in *Don Quixote*. It is now an arts and crafts centre. The **Museo Municipal de Bellas Artes** has works by Córdoban artists and the better-known Zurbarán, Goya, Murillo and Valdés Leál. The very popular **Museo Julio Romero de Torres** takes its name from an artist who painted Córdoba and its women in the early part of this century. Wrought-iron balconies are a special feature of the brick

The Reales Alcázares in Seville contains many examples of such material. Partial restoration continues on the huge site.

Accommodation

Córdoba's expectation of a deluge of visitors spilling over from Expo'92 has inspired the building of new hotels. Three well-established ones:

Parador Nacional, Avenida de la Arruzafa (tel: (957) 27 59 00), 4-star, 188 capacity. Big rooms, gardens and pool in quiet residential area.

Meliá Córdoba, Jardines de la Victoria (tel: (957) 29 80 66), 4-star, 200 capacity. Good service and comfort in pleasant downtown location.

Maimónides, Calle Torrijos 4, (tel: (957) 47 15 00), 3-star, 152 capacity. Close to the mosque and old quarter.

Restaurants

Be sure to visit a bar to try a *copa* of *fino* from Montilla, with which you will usually get a tapa. The best choice of eating places is in the old quarter.

El Caballo Rojo, Calle Cardenal Herrero 28 (tel: (957) 47 53 75). Regional dishes include some Mozarabe specialities.

Confederación de Peñas, Calle Conde Luque 3. Simple food at a low price.

Shopping

Córdoba is well-known for its *Cordobanes* (leatherwork), jewellery and other works in silver and gold, califar pottery and the making of guitars. In the **Zoco** craftspeople have workshops around a courtyard. In the Plaza de la Corredera there is a daily fleamarket.

façades of the arcaded **Plaza de la Corredera**, built in the 17th century. In the handsome **Museo Arqueológico** you can see a rich collection from prehistory to baroque. The **Palacio de los Marqueses de Viana** is a palatial town house with 14 patios; and this beguiling city has many more museums, churches, streets, squares and monuments to intrigue and delight visitors. Abderraman III ordered the building of **Medina Azahara** just five and a half miles (9 km) west of Córdoba, to be the world's most splendid palace-city. Its glory was brief for it was sacked by Berber mercenaries in 1010, and for centuries its stones were used for building elsewhere.

Special Events

May is a month of continuous celebration, with **Cruces de Mayo** (when decorated crosses adorn public places); **Romeria de la Virgen de Linares** (a pilgrimage); the Patio Competition (many private patios are opened for visits); and the **Feria de Mayo** (shows, flamenco, bullfights). The **Corpus Christi** celebration in May or June is among the most renowned in Spain.

◆◆◆
COTO DE DOÑANA (Huelva)

56 miles (90 km) southwest to El Acebuche (via Huelva autovía and El Rocio)
See **Peace and Quiet**.

◆◆
ÉCIJA

55 miles (89 km) east
Tourist brochures call it 'the town of sun and towers' but it is also known as 'the frying pan of Andalucía' because summer temperatures often go above 112° Fahrenheit (45° Centigrade) in the shade. Of towers there are certainly many: 11 of them and 15 belfries. The **Plaza de España** is surrounded by good looking buildings and is popularly known as *el Salón* (sitting room) which is easily understood once you see the many, many retired and unemployed, landless men sitting around. Parts of the **Palacio de Marqués de Peñalflor** can be visited; two other notable Renaissance *palacios* are those of the **Conde de Vallehermoso** and **Valverde**. The **Palacio de Benarmeji**, a National Monument, was built in the 18th century and has a marble front. It is occupied by the military, but the soldier on duty may allow you to see the stables (with a collection of horse carriages) and the central patio. A stroll around the town will take in its more notable churches: **Santa María, Santa Inés, Las Descalzas, Santa Bárbara** and **San Juan Bautista**, which boasts the most impressive tower.

Accommodation

For an overnight stay and food: **Ciudad del Sol**, Calle Cervantes 42 (tel: (957) 483 0300), 2-star, 48 rooms. It has air conditioning, very welcome in the hot months.

◆
ESTEPA

70 miles (113 km) east
Uphill through narrow streets lined by pristine whitewashed houses with black iron window grills and balconies, you reach the **Convento de Santa Clara**, built in 1598. It has a notable altarpiece showing the transition from Plateresque to baroque. Try to see its patio and buy sweets from the nuns. Adjoining is the 15th-century fortress church of **Santa María de la Asunción**. From the **Balcón de Andalucía**, the view is across the rooftops of Estepa to La Campiña, the rich agricultural plain of Seville province. Built in the 18th century and now a National Monument, the **Torre de la Victoria** rises to 160 feet (48m) and is reckoned to be among the most beautiful towers in Andalucía.

Shopping

Sweet, shortcake type biscuits, *polvorones*, or *mantecados* and *roscos*, are what Estepa is famed for. They are especially popular around Christmas.

GRANADA

155 miles (250 km) southeast
Busy with life as a market town
and commercial city, enlivened
by being an important cultural
and conference centre, and
home of Spain's third largest
university, the pomegranate city
has attractions rooted in both
past and present. Monuments,
museums, exhibitions, concerts,
theatre and a lively nightlife
cater to most tastes. Near by in
the Sierra Nevada, rising high
behind the city, is the modern
and very popular ski resort of
Solynieve. The city of close to
300,000 people sprawls across
three mountain spurs thrusting
into *la Vega de Granada*, one
of the richest agricultural areas
in Spain.

Granada, occupied by both
Romans and Visigoths, rose to
prominence with the Moors.
During the 11th century it broke
with Córdoba's caliphacy to
create its own kingdom and,
under the Nasrid dynasty
(1246–1492), Granada
developed into one of Western
Europe's most cultured, artistic
and influential cities.

The sprawling palace of **La
Alhambra** is a magnificent
reminder of the city's past glory.
Many, not only *Granadinos*,
proclaim it as the 'eighth wonder
of the world'. Fine arabesque
traceries, coloured mosaics, cool
colonnades and sparkling
fountains greet the visitor at
every turn. Delicate Nasrid
architecture, stunning
workmanship and sensitive
restoration combine to make the
Alhambra the most important
medieval Arab palace in the
world today. Beside it stands the
contrastingly austere
16th-century **Palacio de Carlos
V**. A little higher up the hill lies
the Nasrid kings' summer
palace, **El Generalife**, with its
shady avenues, water gardens,
fountains and airy gazebos.
Across the Río Darro on the
lower slopes of the opposite hill,
the **Albaicín** quarter has twisted
back streets where behind high
walls many a mansion hides
delightful patios and gardens,
with lofty belvederes to show
what is happening beyond their
seclusion. Higher up is
Sacromonte, traditional home of
cave-dwelling gypsies.
Boabdil, King of Granada and
last Moorish ruler in the
Peninsula, handed the keys of
his city to *los Reyes Católicos*,
and their troops entered
Granada in January 1492. They
later chose the city as their
burial place, and ordered the
construction of the **Capilla Real**,
which should not be missed for
the richness of its decoration and
collection of Italian, Flemish and
Spanish paintings. The huge
Catedral was begun in Gothic
style in 1521, continued in
Renaissance style and finally
completed in the early 18th
century. The artist, architect,
painter and sculptor Alonso
Cano contributed a good deal to
its decoration. Two monasteries
in contrasting styles should also
be seen: **San Jeronimo**
(Renaissance) and **La Cartuja**
(baroque). Other places to visit
include **El Bañuelo**, 11th-century
Moorish baths; the **Museo
Arqueológico** in nearby Casa
Castril, which boasts a
Plateresque façade; and **Casa**

EXCURSIONS FROM SEVILLE

Museo Manuel de Falla, the mansion of one of Spain's greatest composers. Check what is on in the **Palacio de la Madraza**, a cultural centre in what was once an Arab university. Just out of town is the **Museo de Federico García Lorca**, commemorating the Granada-born playwright and poet murdered by the Nationalists during the Civil War.

Accommodation

Hotels are being renovated and new ones built in anticipation of the 1995 World Skiing championships. Close to the Alhambra are:

Parador Nacional de San Francisco (tel: (958) 22 14 00), 4-star, 74 capacity. Once a convent where the bodies of *los Reyes Católicos* rested for a time, it is one of the most popular paradors in Spain. Booking well in advance is essential.

Alhambra Palace (tel: (958) 22 14 68), 4-star, 267 capacity. Mock-Moorish.

América (tel: (958) 22 74 71), 1-star, 21 capacity, open March to October.

For a mountain retreat open all year there is the **Parador Nacional Sierra Nevada**, Carretera de Sierra (tel: (958) 48 02 00), 3-star, 82 capacity.

Restaurants

For a choice of eating places, look in the back streets around the cathedral, Plaza Bibarrambla and Plaza Nueva.

Los Leones, Acera del Darro 10 (tel: (958) 25 50 05), is one of Granada's oldest restaurants,

Water everywhere makes the Alhambra a kind of paradise

offering Andaluz cooking and Granadine specialities.

Sevilla, Calle Oficios 12 (tel: (958) 22 12 23), once a rendezvous for people like García Lorca and Manuel de Falla, serves imaginative regional dishes and charcoal-cooked meats.

Shopping

Granada is well known for its embroidery, lace, ceramics, copperwork and marquetry Also look out for carpets, guitars and leather goods. Behind the 14th-century façade of the Corral de Carbón is an interesting crafts centre. Once site of an Arab silk market, the Alcaicería is now a modern precinct for souvenirs and trinkets.

Special Events

Granada's **Semana Santa** processions count among Spain's finest. During June and July the city hosts its highly regarded **International Festival of Music and Dance** in the Generalife and Palacio de Carlos V.

◆
HUELVA

58 miles (94 km) west
Around 150,000 *onubenses*—as Huelva people are called—inhabit the industrial and port city, which has little involvement with tourism. It is known that the Phoenicians had a settlement named Onuba from which today's citizens get their nickname; the Moors called it Ghelbah (from which Huelva is derived); and after the Christian Reconquest it lived in the shadow of Seville. The English-style **Barrio Reina Victoria**, which the Rio Tinto Company

built for its workers in 1917, is one of the city's most notable 'sights'. But what brings most visitors close to the city is the proximity of places related to Cristóbal Colón (see **Palos de la Frontera**), and the **Monumento a Colón**, a grandiose sculpture by Gertrude Whitney at Punta del Sebo, where the estuaries of the Odiel and Tinto rivers meet. It was a gift from the United States in 1929.

The **Museo Provincial** has objects relating to neolithic and Tartessian times.

Accommodation
Tartessos, Avenida Martín Alonso Pinzón 13 (tel: (955) 24 56 11), 3-star, 102 rooms.

Restaurant
La Cazuela, Calle García Fernández 5 (tel: (955) 25 80 96). Basque and Andalucian cuisine; recommended.

ITÁLICA
6 miles (9 km) northwest
Founded by Scipio Africanus as a settlement for his legionaries, this was among the earliest Roman towns in the Peninsula. It quickly grew in size and importance, and Emperors Trajan (AD52–177) and Hadrian (AD76–138) were born here. Excavations have revealed a large amphitheatre, forum and villas of the wealthy with good mosaics, and there is a small museum.

Special Events
Each summer the **Itálica Festival International de Danza** is held here under the auspices of the Diputación de Sevilla and the Luis Cernuda Fundación.

JEREZ DE LA FRONTERA
60 miles (97 km) southwest
Jerez is derived from 'Xeres', the Moorish name of the town; 'de la Frontera' denotes it was for some time a Christian frontier town on the boundary with Muslim Spain. On the bedrock of sherry and brandy production, it has long been among Spain's most commercially successful towns. It intends keeping things that way by increasing profitability within its traditional activities and developing other revenue sources, such as tourism. The airport (Aeropuerto de la Para) is being extended. As you approach the town it looks modern, and many of its 180,000 inhabitants occupy new apartment blocks. But the very attractive old quarter is still its heart; the old Anglo-Andaluz sherry dynasties still wield the social influence and economic power, in spite of the arrival of multinational corporations and opposing politicians; the old traditions are still strong and some are growing stronger.

Jerez—Pura Andalucía is the town's promotional slogan, and it is true that in Jerez many of the idealised images of this region come alive. There are rich land barons, grand *palacios* and large *fincas* (estates), finely bred horses and fighting bulls, lively or passionate flamenco, beautiful women and handsome men, and much flowing wine.

Visits to sherry *bodegas* can be made in the mornings from Monday to Friday, but many are closed during August. One example is **Williams and Humbert**, Calle Nuño de Caña, which has tours at 10.30, 12.00 and 13.30 hrs. Information about visiting others can be obtained from the tourist office. Another excellent reason to journey to Jerez is the **Real Escuela Andaluza del Arte Ecuestre**, Recrea de las Cadenas, Avenida Duque de Abrantes: check in Seville for the times of the unique performance of an equestrian ballet, with Spanish music and costumes from the 17th century. From Monday to Friday, (except Thursday) from 11.00 to 13.00 hrs, visits can be made to the stables and training sessions. Also in the city, one of the most fascinating collections of timepieces to be seen in Europe is on display in the **Museo de Relojes**.

A wander through the old town does not take long and there is much to see. Start in Plaza de la Asunción where the 16th-century **Casa del Cabildo Viejo** (old town hall) houses a small archaeological museum and library. Here too is the 15th-century Gothic-Mudéjar **Iglesia de San Dioniso**, patron saint of Jerez. The **Alcázar-Mezquita** was built in the 12th century as a residence for the caliph of Seville, and its mosque was converted into a church. Among many other churches, the most notable are **San Salvador, San Miguel** and **Iglesia-Convento de Santo Domingo**, where exhibitions are often held in the cloisters. Near by is one of the finest mansions of

Celebrating the horse at the Feria del Caballo in Jerez

a sherry dynasty, **Palacio Domecq**. Just out of town on the road to Medina Sidonia is the monumental ensemble of **Cartuja de Santa María de la Defensión**, a monastery founded in 1476, which is inhabited by a silent order. The impressive front is in Greco-Roman style; the Gothic church was completed in the 18th century.

Accommodation

There is a fair choice of places to stay in Jerez. El Puerto de Santa María and Arcos de la Frontera are also convenient towns for the area (see separate entries).
Jerez, Avenida Alvaro Domecq 35 (tel: (956) 30 06 00), 5-star, 121 rooms. Luxury at a better price than comparable places in Seville. Gardens and pool.

Avenida Jerez, Avenida Alvaro Domecq 10 (tel: (956) 34 74 11), 3-star, 95 rooms, garage. Modern and more than adequate at half the price.
San Martín, Calle Caballeros 28 (tel: (956) 33 70 40), 1-star pension, 10 rooms. Cosy and welcoming.

Restaurants and Bars

You can eat well and cheaply in Jerez: bars, good and plentiful, serve mostly fish and ham based tapas and raciones and there are quite a few *freidurías de pescado*, like **El Boquerón de Plata** on Plaza de Santiago, for freshly fried Atlantic fish. Among the best restaurants for local fare are: **Tenido 6**, Calle Circo 10 (tel: (956) 34 48 35); **El Bosque**, Avenida Alvaro Domecq (tel: (956) 30 70 30); **Venta Antonio**, 3 miles (5 km) on Sanlúcar road (tel: (956) 33 05 35).
For a drink, try fashionable **Bora Bora**, Calle Sevilla 22, and for flamenco of the spontaneous sort, go around midnight to **Camino del Rocío**, Calle Velázquez, Polígono San Benito.

Shopping

Sherry and brandy are obvious good buys; so is vinegar. Bodegas offer good prices.

Special Events

Jerez enjoys itself very much at its two biggest annual celebrations, to which people come from far and wide: **Feria del Caballo** (end of April/early May), when horses are the centre of attraction; and the **Fiesta de la Vendimia**, during the week leading up to 24 September, when the grape harvest is blessed and a different sherry-consuming country each year is the theme of the festivities. Jerez's Grand Prix circuit hosts the Spanish event in September, and the new Olympic-standard athletics track is the venue for international events.

◆◆
MATALASCAÑAS AND MAZAGÓN
58 miles (94 km) southwest to Matalascañas via El Rocio; 70 miles (112 km) west to Mazagón via Palos de Frontera
Relatively recent and rapid development has created these two popular summer resorts along Huelva's **Costa de la Luz** (Coast of Light) which has superb beaches, among the best in Europe. They are long and wide and have fine, golden sand, backed by dunes in some places and by pinewoods in others. The two resorts are 18 miles (29 km) apart along a road through pinewoods, and both are good bases for visiting the Coto de Doñana National Park (see **Peace and Quiet**).
Mazagón is a resort which has more charm and is more family oriented.

Accommodation
Local travel and property agents can advise about accommodation in other hotels or in apartments. The most interesting place to stay is on a clifftop near Mazagón: **Parador Nacional Cristóbal Colón**, Carretera Mazagón–Moguer (tel: (955) 37 60 00), 3-star, 43 rooms. Recently refurbished and very comfortable, with pleasant gardens and a pool and views of the beach.

◆◆
OSUNA
61 miles (98 km) east
Osuna has the best preserved and maintained old quarter of Seville's provincial towns. The first Duke of Osuna was given his title in 1562, making the town the fiefdom of one of Spain's most influential aristocratic families. When their power was at its height through the 17th and 18th centuries, they and their followers endowed the town with many beautiful buildings. Take a walk along **Calle San Pedro** to see the fine houses of this period. The Plateresque **Panteón Ducal** is still used as the final resting places for the bones of family members. It is part of the Renaissance **Iglesia Colegial de Santa María de la Asunción**, which has been declared a National Monument for the importance of its architecture and wealth of interior decoration. The **Monasterio de la Encarnación** has a museum with valuable religious art and artefacts. The **Antigua Universidad**, an imposing building of the 16th century, is now a school. Once part of the town wall, the **Torre del Agua** houses an archaeological museum displaying Iberian and Roman remains.

◆◆
PALOS DE LA FRONTERA
62 miles (100 km) west
By an edict of *los Reyes Católicos*, Palos was charged with providing Cristóbal Colón with ships, men and provisions. **Calle Colón 34** is the home of the Pinzón brothers who undertook the task and served as captains on the voyage. It was in the

Iglesia de San Jorge that Colón and his crew prayed for their wellbeing, and at La Fontanilla, with a well in its garden, that the small fleet's water was drawn. The wharf from which the *Santa María, Pinta* and *Niña* departed on 3 August 1492 no longer exists, as the river here has long been silted up. The **Monasterio de La Rábida**, a Gothic-Mudéjar complex, has been home to Franciscan monks since the beginning of the 15th century. Monks show visitors around the building where Colón sought respite and sustenance for himself and his son, Diego, and where he was aided by the friars Antonio de Marchena and Juan Pérez in his petitions to *los Reyes Católicos*. Murals done by Vázquez Díaz in 1930 depict the 'discovery' of America.

Accommodation

Hostería de La Rábida (tel: (955) 35 03 12) 3-star, 5 rooms. A good place to stay and to eat, next to the monastery and operated in parador-style by the Diputacíon de Huelva.

◆◆
EL PUERTO DE SANTA MARÍA

68 miles (109 km) southwest
Rival to Jerez as another town with sherry as its economic base, El Puerto does not have much in the way of monumental buildings except for its **Castillo de San Marcos** and **Iglesia de Prioral Mayor**. But it does have sherry bodegas to visit and many good places to enjoy the wine and freshly caught seafood. It also offers a good choice of hotels, pleasant beaches, facilities for watersports and golf, as well as the attraction of luxury

developments like Puerto Sherry. Its nightlife is livelier than in Jerez and attracts many Sevillanos over weekends, as well as Americans from the nearby Rota naval base.
Osborne's bodega, Calle Fernán Caballero 3, can be visited Monday to Friday 10.30–13.30 hrs; and there are others open to the public.

Accommodation

Monasterio San Miguel, Calle Larga 27 (tel: (956) 86 11 40), 4-star, 258 capacity, garage. A successful conversion of an old monastery into a modern hotel, this is a delightful place to stay and well priced for what it offers. Swimming pool.
In Puerto Sherry,
Puerto Sherry Yacht Club (tel: (956) 87 37 07), 4-star, 105 capacity. Double the price, modern, with full facilities. Swimming pool.
Sherry, Calle Veneroni 1 (tel: (956) 87 08 52), 1-star pension, 24 capacity. Homely, at the other end of the scale.

Restaurants and Bars

Along the riverside, Ribera del Río is lined with bars and restaurants. Here you can do *el tapeo* and try **Casa Flores**, number 9 (tel: (956) 86 35 12) for an excellent seafood meal.
Alboronia, Calle Santo Domingo 24 (tel: (956) 86 16 09). Señor Solano runs a smart restaurant in a typical Andalucian house with an interior garden. The cooking is imaginative and uses the best of local produce.
Joy Sherry, Carretera de Sanlúcar, a multi-space disco amid luxuriant gardens, is very animated in summer.

PEACE AND QUIET

Wildlife and Countryside in and around Seville
by Paul Sterry

Within a comparatively short distance of Seville, visitors can find everything from stunning coastline to high sierras, pine woodland and marshes. Flowers grow in profusion in the spring and, for the birdwatcher, few areas in Europe can rival the range of species to be found. The sierras offer a wide variety of mountain birds, while the Coto de Doñana, to the southwest, is considered to be the finest area of wetland left in Europe. Seville also lies close to one of the most important migration routes for European birds. Millions pass over the Straits of Gibraltar each spring and autumn and the countryside can be alive with birds.

In and Around Seville

Although not renowned as a haven for wildlife, the city still offers a few opportunities for birdwatching. Although seemingly lifeless during the height of summer, leafy parks and gardens can be full of songbirds in spring. Swifts and swallows hunt for insects in the skies above and larger birds pass over on migration.
Away from the centre of the city, visitors are likely to see and hear serins singing in parks and gardens which have plenty of leafy cover. These birds are Europe's smallest finches, and are best identified by their bright yellow rumps. The

Sea holly is well adapted to survive the roughest weather

PEACE AND QUIET

jingling song is attractive and reminiscent of the canary, to which they are related. In spring, several species of warbler and sometimes even nightingales can be found in quiet spots.

Look for crested larks feeding beside the roads on the outskirts of the city, often in the most unpromising locations. Hoopoes are also occasionally seen feeding close to busy roads, and birdwatchers, since birds may be pushed close to shore. Seabirds sometimes pass close to beaches, but it is generally headlands, such as Cape Trafalgar, that provide the best opportunities for seawatching. Stabilised sand dunes support a riot of flowers in the spring and can be really exciting places to explore. Among the most colourful flowers are sea rocket, sea holly, sea medick and cottonweed.

colourful bee-eaters sometimes perch on roadside wires.

The Coast

The Atlantic coast from Tarifa to the Río Guadalquivir is one of the most varied and beautiful in all of southern Spain. In the south, it is rocky with dramatic cliffs, while, further north, there are sandy beaches and dunes.

Not surprisingly, this stretch of coast is frequently battered by southwesterly winds. It is often the roughest weather that is the most rewarding for

Inland from the coast, woodlands cover many of the hillsides. In some areas these are mainly of pine, while elsewhere the cork oaks so characteristic of Andalucia predominate. In open areas of forest, a rich understorey of shrubby plants develops, with tree heathers, strawberry trees, junipers, cistuses and rosemary in abundance. Orchids, narcissi, French lavender and asphodels can be found by careful searching at ground level. Birdlife is rich and varied in the woodland and undergrowth, although the birds themselves are not always easy to see. First thing in the morning is the best time of day for birdwatching, and spring is the best season. Warblers skulk in the cover but may emerge briefly to sing their scratchy songs. Woodlarks are more elegant songsters and the twittering song of the serin is easy to locate.

Hills and Mountains

The low-lying floodplain of the Río Guadalquivir, on which Seville is situated, is flanked to the north and to the southeast by hills and mountains. These sierras provide a dramatic contrast to the lowlands, both in terms of scenery and of wildlife, and are fortunately within easy driving distance of the city.

Bee-eaters really do eat bees, as well as other insects, and can sometimes be seen perched above the roadside

PEACE AND QUIET

When ascending the mountains, visitors pass through a range of vegetation types, from typically Mediterranean scrub at lower levels, through oak and pine forests and finally to bare mountain slopes above.

When heading north to the Sierra Modena or southeast to the Serrania de Ronda, the first part of the journey into the hills passes through areas where olives and mastic trees thrive. A walk through this maquis vegetation will reveal a profusion of other plants, including strawberry tree, caper, tree heather, kermes oak, brooms and gorses.

In spring and summer, butterflies are frequent visitors to nectar-rich flowers, and species such as scarce swallowtails, two-tailed pashas, blues, hairstreaks, fritillaries and clouded yellow are often seen. A typical range of Mediterranean birds can be found in this habitat, with various species of warbler being noticeable.

Higher in the mountains, the pine woods and oak woods have a rich understorey of flowers, many of which also occur at lower altitudes. In addition to more widespread species, visitors may find a good selection of orchids in the spring, particularly under pine trees. Especially noticeable are giant orchids, man orchids and mirror orchids. Each of those really lives up to its name – the giant orchid may reach up to your waist, the man orchid has its petals and sepals arranged in such a way that each flower looks like a tiny figure, and the mirror orchid's lip, or lower

Migratory Birds
One of the highlights of any trip to southern Spain in spring is the arrival of the bee-eaters. These noisy and colourful birds are arguably Spain's most beautiful species. With their bright blue-green, rufous and yellow plumage, they are easy to see, gliding aerobatically in search of insects or perching on overhead wires.

It is the movement of larger birds—storks, cranes and birds of prey in particular—that is the most noticeable aspect of bird migration in southern Spain. From March to May, and again in September and October, thousands of white storks, honey buzzards, black kites and many other species are funnelled through southern Spain. Relying on land-generated thermals, they concentrate towards the tip of Spain in autumn and radiate out from their landfall on the coast in spring.

petal, has a shiny surface. Birds of prey are often seen circling over the woodlands. Eagles, hawks and kestrels are all found within the region.

Ronda

Although mountain birds can be seen almost anywhere at suitable altitudes, a particularly good spot to search for them is around the town of Ronda. The town itself is cut in two by a dramatic gorge, and here lesser kestrels, choughs, crag martins, blue rock thrushes and the occasional griffon vulture can be seen. Further into the mountains, a lot more griffon vultures can be found, along with Egyptian vultures, golden eagles, Bonelli's eagles and peregrines.

Cabo de Trafalgar

The Cabo de Trafalgar coastline is arguably the most dramatic and rugged stretch along the whole of southern Spain. Pounded by the Atlantic, the cliffs and beaches are inspiring whatever the mood of the weather, and the scrub-covered headlands provide opportunities to find both migrant and resident birds.

Seabirds sometimes pass close to the shore during periods of onshore winds. In spring, migrating birds also move along the coast heading north from the southern tip of Spain. Plants to look for include sea daffodil, cistuses, vetches, rosemary and grape hyacinths.

Laguna de Medina

This comparatively small freshwater lake lies close to the C440 near Jerez de la Frontera, south of Seville. There is free access along the shore, using paths and tracks, and a wide range of birds, especially migrant ducks and waders, can be found in spring and autumn. Look for spoonbills and egrets around the margins of the lake. You are not likely to confuse the spoonbill with any other bird; as its name suggests, its long beak has a spoon-shaped end, and anyway the bird is very big,

Not all of southern Spain's coast is busy beaches, as the Cabo de Trafalgar proves

PEACE AND QUIET

Flamingo on the Coto de Doñana

pure white, and has a spiky crest in the breeding season. Those parts of the lake with reed-fringed margins have breeding birds such as Cetti's warblers and great reed warblers. Their songs are loud and far-carrying, but are often drowned by the croaking of thousands of frogs.

Coto de Doñana

The Coto de Doñana, or more precisely the Parque Nacional de Doñana, is one of the finest wetlands in Europe. As well as an extraordinary range of birds, there are also unusual mammals and interesting flowers among the different habitats—reed-beds, marismas (seasonally flooding wetlands), sand dunes and pine woodlands.

Access to the park itself is only by conducted tours, which must be prearranged by contacting the offices of ICONA in Seville or the National Park Centre at El Acebuche (tel: (955) 43 04 32). However, most if not all of the specialities of the Coto de Doñana can be seen around its perimeter. La Rocina information centre, near the village of El Rocio (tel: (955) 40 61 40), gives information about areas adjoining the park which can be visited without guides. There are hides at the La Rocina information centre and at El Acebuche centre; wetland species can also be seen from the bridge at El Rocio and shorebirds on the beach at Matalascañas.

Wetland birds are, without doubt, the highlight of any visit to the Coto de Doñana. Throughout the summer months, the marismas are home to egrets, spoonbills, flamingos, black-winged stilts and avocets. Ducks feed on areas of open water and, for added variety, migration time sees the arrival of a wide range of waders. Even the winter months are not without highlights: thousands of geese and ducks arrive from northern Europe.

Birds of prey are another feature of the Coto de Doñana. Look for vultures, eagles, and kites. If you are really lucky, you might even see an imperial eagle. This majestic bird, distinguished from other eagles by its white shoulders, is now very rare in Spain.

FOOD AND DRINK

Olive oil (*aceite de oliva*) and
garlic (*ajo*), liberally used, are
staple ingredients in basic local
cooking. Tomato (*tomate*), onion
(*cebolla*) and green or red
pepper (*pimiento*) also feature
strongly. Chicken (*pollo*) and
pork (*cerdo*) have traditionally
been the most used meats, but
veal (*ternera*) and beef (*vaca*)
are now widely available. Cured
ham from mountain areas (*jamón
serrano*), by itself or in
combinations with melon or
other ingredients, is among the
most popular snacks and
starters. There is much
discussion and dispute about the
comparative quality of hams
from different areas. Red
paprika sausage (*chorizo*) and
blood sausage (*morcilla*),
delicately flavoured with herbs,
are the most-used prepared
meat products. The big choice of
fish (*pescados*) and shellfish
(*mariscos*) comes from both
Mediterranean and Atlantic
catches, and from the mountain
streams of Seville and
neighbouring provinces. Eggs
(*huevos*) are used hard-boiled
(*duros*) in salads, scrambled
(*revueltos*) or in omelettes
(*tortillas*). Except for potatoes
(*patatas*) and carrots
(*zanahorias*), most vegetables
(*verduras* or *legumbres*) have
traditionally been above-ground
varieties, with an emphasis on
green beans (*judias*), broad
beans (*habas*), peas (*guisantes*)
and chick peas (*garbanzos*); but
the choice has widened in
recent years. Seville province is
an important producer of rice
(*arroz*), the main ingredient for

Baked eggs 'a la flamenca'

the well-known *paella*. In
addition to tomato and onion, the
main ingredients for salads
(*ensaladas*) are cucumber
(*pepino*) and lettuce (*lechuga*).
Andalucía is now a major
producer of avocados
(*aguacates*), which are the base
for many starters and salads.
Desserts (*postres*) and pastries
(*pasteles*) are a delectable
legacy from Moorish times. The
region also produces many
different fruits (*frutas*), including
exotic subtropical varieties.
Cheeses (*quesos*) from other
countries, or local copies, are
more and more available.
Among local varieties, *queso de*

FOOD AND DRINK

Grazalema, a sheep's milk cheese, is ever popular. Traditional cooking is straightforward, with little use made of elaborate sauces. The traditional cooking methods are on a griddle (*a la plancha*), fried (*frito*), grilled (*a la parilla*), baked or roasted (*al horno* or *asado*), or plain-boiled (*cocido*). Since Andalucía achieved regional political autonomy, there has been a revived interest in traditional regional cooking, as part of the general increased promotion and awareness of all that is typically Andaluz. This trend is found in both homes and restaurants. Another trend, shared with other Mediterranean regions, is the adaptation of traditional recipes, or the creation of new ones, to make light dishes which satisfy modern tastes and dietary concerns. Innovative chefs come up with imaginative combinations of whatever is the best of local produce during different seasons.

Some restaurants provide menu translations, and more will probably do so to help the increased number of foreign visitors attracted by the publicity around Expo'92. A few dishes which you are very likely to come across and ought to try, are: *boquerones*, fresh fried anchovies; *cabito* or *choto*, kid goat; *callos a la andaluza* or *el menudo*, a tripe stew which visitors often order in ignorance; *cocido*, Spain's 'national' dish—a stew of beans, chick peas, potatoes, rice and meat; *croquetas*, potato croquettes

Fish fried to perfection

which sometimes include chicken; *ensalada de Sevilla*, endives and olives with tarragon; *gambas al pil-pil*, prawns cooked in spices, garlic and oil; *gazpacho Andaluz*, a healthy and refreshing 'liquid salad' or cold soup of tomato, cucumber, onion, green pepper, garlic, bread, oil and vinegar; *helados*, ice creams, popular throughout the day and as a dessert in this hot climate; *huevos a la flamenca*, baked eggs, ham, spicy sausage, beans, peas, onions, garlic and tomato; *menestra*, mixed vegetables in season; *migas*, breadcrumbs fried in oil and garlic with a variety of garnishes; *pato a la sevillana*, duck, bacon, peppers and olives; *pescao* or *pescato frito*, fresh fish quick-fried in very hot olive oil; *polvorones*, shortcake biscuits; *rabo de toro*, oxtail which is sometimes prepared with hot pepper; *riñones a la Jerezana*, kidneys in sherry; *sopa de picadillo*, a soup of chick peas, ham, chicken, potato, rice and egg; *ternera a la sevillana*, veal or beef and olives cooked in white wine; *torrijas*, for dessert, bread soaked in milk, battered, fried and sweetened with honey; *tortas de aceite*, flat cakes; and *zarzuela*, mixed fish stew.

Tapas

The word *tapas* comes from *tapar* (to cover). Traditionally, glasses were covered with a small plate and it became the custom in bars to put a snack on it.

Olives (*aceitunas*), nuts (*nuezes*) and potato crisps (*patatas fritas*) are the simplest tapas, usually served free with a beer, wine or sherry. But tapas can be small portions of almost any type of food in a variety of preparations, simple or elaborate. They are usually displayed on the bar counter and you order, and pay for, what you want. Bars in Seville compete keenly for custom with the quality and delectability of their tapas. Doing *el tapeo*, going from bar to bar to sample tapas, is very much part of the city's eating habits, and it is an essential Sevillan experience for visitors. *Raciones* are larger portions.

Eating Times and Places

Breakfast (*desayuno*) is light—usually coffee (*café*) or a chocolate drink (*chocolate* or *cacao*) with toast (*tostada*) or pastries (*pasteles*). This is widely available in bars, and is often repeated during the morning. Lunch (*almuerzo*) is traditionally the main meal of the day, and starts after 14.00hrs. It is usually preceded by an *aperitivo*. Around 18.00hrs, a *merienda* is taken—more coffee and pastries. After work (from about 20.00hrs), it is time for drinks and tapas. The evening meal at home is light, and is taken after 22.00hrs. Around this time restaurants are getting busy with people wanting dinner (*cena*).

At lunchtime restaurants offer a *menu del día*—a fixed-price menu. In basic eateries this can be fair value for filling food. In more sophisticated places it is often an unsatisfactory compromise and you can do better by choosing well from the menu (*carta*). Many restaurants are closed on Sunday evenings and on Mondays or another day

in the week, and during August
for their annual holiday.
Restaurants are graded with one
to five forks, but this reflects the
standard of facilities, not
necessarily the cooking.
From before lunchtime to late at
night, going to a bar (or bars) for
a selection of tapas or a racion is
an obvious alternative to eating
at a restaurant. There are also
cocederos or *freidurías de
pescado*: basic places serving
freshly fried fish with wine or
beer in the evenings. Seville has
the usual big city eating places
as well: fast-food cafeterias,
chicken grill and other
takeaways, international
franchise operators, and 'milk
bars' (*granjas*).

Wine

Wine is *vino*; red is *tinto*, rosé is
rosado, and white is *blanco*.
Wines from Rioja and Penedés,
the best-known wine regions of
Spain, are widely available, as
are those of other controlled

*Some of the best food can be
found in local bars*

wine-producing areas,
Denominaciones de Origen or
DOs. Many villages have a
bodega producing *vino terreno*
(wine of the land) for local
consumption. It can often be
strong and heady but is always
cheap and flows freely during
the many *fiestas*. Málaga's sweet
and luscious wine has long been
a British favourite. Cádiz
province produces the
renowned sherries (see below),
and the Montilla-Moriles area of
Córdoba province is another
producer of *vinos generosos*
(wines which are high in alcohol)
for drinking before or after a
meal. Good white table wines
now also come from Montilla-
Moriles as well as Cádiz and
Huelva provinces. Most
restaurants have a house wine
(*vino de la casa*) and will usually
offer their own region's wines.
Excellent quality and value can

be enjoyed among the choice of *cava*, sparkling wine produced by the champagne method in the Penedés area of Catalunya.

Sherry

Sherry takes its name from Xeres, the Moorish name for Jerez de la Frontera, where sherry originated and is still made. It is known locally as *vino de Jerez*. The very chalky soil in this area of Cádiz province favours the grape types (Palomino, Pedro Ximénez and Moscatel) mainly used for sherry. Production is centred on Jerez de la Frontera, Puerto de Santa María and Sanlúcar de Barrameda, where big *bodegas* (which can be visited—see **Excursions**) use the *solera* system to mature the wine and maintain consistency of taste. Four barrels are laid one above another, and mature wine drawn from the bottom barrel is replaced by putting new wine in the top barrel, to be filtered through the system over a period of years. Expert blending by the cellarman (*capataz*) ensures bottled sherries of uniform taste and quality for the different types. *Fino* is very pale and dry; *amontillado* is a fuller, nuttier and older fino; *oloroso* is similar but darker and more fragrant. *Palos cortados* is halfway between an *amontillado* and *oloroso*, and is rarely available; cream sherries are sweet, either pale and light-tasting or dark and velvety; *manzanilla*, only made in Sanlúcar, is like fino. Slightly varying shapes of tapering glasses (*copitas*) are used for different types of sherry.

Other drinks—alcoholic

Almost every other conceivable alcoholic drink is available at all hours, and usually served in more generous measure and at lower prices than in other European countries. Be warned—it is easy to over-indulge if you are used to smaller measures and more restricted licensing hours. The strength of ordinary Spanish beer (*cerveza*) is between 4.6 and 5.4 per cent alcohol per volume. *Una caña* (from the tap) is usually cheaper than bottled beer. Jerez de la Frontera is a big producer of brandy (*coñac* or *jerez*). There is also a wide choice of liqueurs and the full range of imported spirits and beers. *Sangría* is a mixture of soda water, red wine, brandy, fruit juices and ice. Again beware: it can be very intoxicating!

Other drinks—non-alcoholic

Drinkable water from a tap or fountain is called *agua potable*. Good water may cause a reaction if it is unfamiliar, however, so you will probably do best to drink a bottled water, with or without gas (*agua mineral*, *con gas* or *sin gas*). Tea (*té*) is most often served with a slice of lemon (*limón*). Hot camomile tea (*infusión de manzanilla*) is both refreshing and supposedly calming. A cool drink made from ground nuts (*horchata*) is wholesome and refreshing, but an acquired taste.

Freshly prepared and iced fruit juices (*granizados*) help slake the thirst on a hot summer day. There is also a big choice of fruit juices (*zumos*) available in

FOOD AND DRINK

bottles, cans and cartons. Check the ingredients if you want 100 per cent fruit juice. Fresh milk (*leche del día*) is now widely available. Then there is coffee (*café*), which is black expresso unless you specifically ask for *con leche* (with milk), *grande* (large with milk) or one of many other different styles on offer.

Where to Eat

The selection of tapas bars and restaurants which follows is just that—a selection. Many other places justify inclusion, and many new places will be opening, in the city and on the Expo'92 site. As well as suggesting specific places, this list leads you into streets and areas where there are other eateries, and gives an idea of the sort of places you can find in Seville. Tapas bars are listed under different areas; restaurants are also listed by area and then briefly described in the listing by the type of cuisine available.

Central Seville

Tapas bars **El Rinconcillo**, Gerona 2: tasty tapas of *espinacas* (spinach), *pavías* (battered cod fish) and a variety of rice-based snacks can be enjoyed in this centuries-old bar which is loaded with atmosphere. **La Mina**, Cuesta del Rosario 9 has been going since 1910: *caracoles* (snails) are the favourites in this bodega. **El Trasiego**, Harinas 8, has wines from around the world and a choice of local cheeses. **El Patio**, San Eloy 9, serves a special black beer and gets very packed in the evening with a mixed and animated crowd.

See restaurant listings by type of cuisine for: **L'Arroz**, Calle Juan A Cavestany 6; **Barca de Don Raimundo**, Calle Placentines 25; **Casa Robles**, Calle Alvarez Quintero 58; **Don Raimundo**, Argote de Molina 26; **Egaña-Oriza** Calle San Fernando 41; **El Figon del Cabildo**, Plaza del Cabildo; **Enrique Becerra**, Calle Gamazo 2; **Hang Zhou**, Calle Mateos Gago 5; **La Mandragora**, Calle Albuera 11; **Llorens**, Calle Pastor y Landero 19.

Barrio de Santa Cruz

Tapas bars **Casa Román**, Plaza de Los Venerables, has long been one of the most popular tapas bars in the barrio, and is known for its *jamón Ibérico*. In the same plaza, **Santa Cruz** also does good tapas, and its restaurant is equally recommended for Andaluz dishes.

See restaurant listings by type of cuisine for: **Café Copenhague**, Calle Vida; **El 3 de Oro**, Calle Santa María de la Blanca 34; **La Albahaca**, Plaza de Santa Cruz; **La Judería**, Calle Cano y Cueto 13.

Calle Betis

This street along the west bank of the Río Guadalquivir, and adjoining Triana, has a big choice of different eateries. Among its bars, **La Primera del Puente**, number 66, serves *pavías* and *pinchitos* (small kebabs) as appetising tapas.

See restaurant listings by type of cuisine for: **Asador Ox's**, 61; **Chino International**, 41; **Crêperie Cibeles**, 40; **O'Mamma Mia**, 33; **Río Grande**, 70.

In **Triana**
Tapas bars **Bodega Mantua**,
Pagés del Corro 45 is one of the
old-style bars of the area.
Caracoles are a speciality among
traditional tapas. On the same
street: **La Esquina**, corner of
Calle Pureza, where *cola de toro*
(bull's tail) is the speciality; **El
Tamboril**, number 43, is homely
in its cooking and atmosphere;
Mesón La Cava, 82, serves
tempting *pinchitos*; **Albahaca**,
119, has a good choice of local
specialities. At **Casa Cuesta**,
Calle Castilla 1, the favourite is
menudo (bits of veal, ham,
chorizo and chick peas in white
wine). In the adjoining restaurant
the recommended dish is *rabo
de toro*. More bars line the
street, including dingy **Sol y
Sombra**, number 151, where the

walls are papered with old
bullfighting posters. **Ruperto**,
Calle Santa Cecilia 2, does a
roaring trade in *cordonices*
(quails); and another place to try
on the same street is **Casa Diego**,
number 29. **Avenida**, Avenida
Alvar Nuñez 12, does *pimientos*
and *pulpo* (octopus) in various
ways. Other good bars on the
same street are: **Los Angeles**,
number 12; **El Valle**, 18;
Cortegana, 22.
See restaurant listings by type of
cuisine for: **El Ancora**, Calle
Virgen de la Huerta; **Pello
Roteta**, Calle Farmacéutico
Herrera 10; **La Loncha**, Pureza
104; **Pleamar**, Calle Gustavo
Bacarisas 1; **Trastevere**, Calle
Salado 6.

In the Barrio de Santa Cruz

FOOD AND DRINK

Los Remedios

Tapas bars **José Luis**, Plaza de
Cuba 3, is a luxurious place with
bull-based décor and good, but
rather pricey, tapas. **La Tasca**,
Calle Montecarmelo 4, is among
the most popular bars in the
district because of its choice of
good tapas. **El Picadero**, Calle
Madre Rafols 6, is another
favourite with a wide selection.
Los Latinos, Calle Virgen de la
Estrella 2, offers hams and a
number of vegetable tapas. **Los
Mellizos**, Calle Virgen de las
Montañas, has *bombas* (potatoes
with meat filling) as its speciality.
See restaurant listings by type of
cuisine for: **Anthony's**, Calle
Virgen de las Montañas 2; **La
Dorada**, Virgen de Agua Santas 6;
Sloppy Joe's, Calle Asunción 62;
Tel Aviv, Calle Virgen de la
Estrella 23; **Woody Moon**, Calle
Virgen de Luján.

American

Sloppy Joe's, Asunción 62 (tel:
427 6483). Pizzas, hamburgers,
salads, sandwiches. The décor is
a mix of American and typical
Andaluz.
Woody Moon, Calle Virgen de
Luján 31 (tel: 428 1909). New
Yorker style eatery serving
hamburgers, sandwiches, pizzas
and Tex-Mex specialities.
Imported music.

Andalucian

La Albahaca, Plaza de Santa
Cruz (tel: 422 0714). In a house
dating from the early part of this
century, two rooms have
ceramic tiling of the time and are
decorated in typical Sevillan
style. Andaluz favourites and
other dishes are served. Stylish,
with attentive service, prices are
relatively high.

Casa Robles, Alvarez Quintero
58 (tel: 421 3150). Usually
humming with a talkative cross-
section of Sevillanos, who come
here for unpretentious cooking
of good quality ingredients at
moderate prices.
Don Raimundo, Argote de
Molina 26 (tel: 422 3355). This
efficient and moderately priced
restaurant, furnished with
antiques and decorated in
baroque style, presents both
traditional Andaluz and modern
creative cooking.
Enrique Becerra, Calle Gamazo
2 (tel: 422 7093). Typical
Andalucian décor and dishes at
moderate prices.
El Figon del Cabildo, Arfe
19/Plaza del Cabildo (tel: 422
0117). The mostly Andaluz menu
also has other dishes like the
Castilian favourite, *cordero
lechal asado* (roast baby lamb).
Big and efficient with fair prices,
but the cooking is nothing
special. Much used by tour
groups.
La Judería, Calle Cano y Cueto
13 (tel: 441 2052). Its slogan 'The
Art of Gastronomy and the
Miracle of Communication', says
something about this place's
serious cooking but slight
pretension. There is a good
choice of well-prepared and
presented seafoods and meats.
Prices are moderate.
Llorens, Calle Pastor y Landero
19 (tel: 456 1056). Bernardo
Clemente's recently renovated
restaurant occupies an old
private palacio, and is now in the
vanguard of Seville design and
cooking. In both there is a
harmonious meeting of the
classic and very modern. Prices
are most satisfying for a

memorable dining experience.
La Loncha, Calle Pureza 104 (tel:
427 1824). Here you can partake
of game and the most classic
Andaluz dishes at reasonable
prices. Hunting and shooting
features in the interior décor and
there is a pleasant patio for
warm-weather dining.

Basque

Asador Ox's Betis 61 (tel: 427
9585). The Egaña family entered
the Seville restaurant business
with this simple and functional
place, where waitresses give
efficient and friendly service.
The family ensures that high
standards are maintained in the
quality meat dishes, prepared in
Basque–Navarran styles (mostly
grilled), and offered at
reasonable prices.
Egaña-Oriza, San Fernando 41
(tel: 422 7211). Basque cooking
ranks among the very best in

Spain, and here the Egaña family
offers both Basque and gourmet
international cooking of the
highest standard. The spacious
and very elegant restaurant
adjoins the Jardines Murillo. Its
Bar España is equally stylish,
with good tapas and a terrace
from which to watch passing
people (and traffic). Prices may
appear a little high, but taking all
into account they are fair.
Pello Roteta, Farmacéutico
Herrera 10 (tel: 427 8417). This
family-run place is tastefully
decorated in pastel tones, the
tables are big and well spaced,
the lighting is relaxing and the
service is attentive. Prices are
moderate for the traditional and
new-style Basque dishes.

Chinese

Chino International, Calle Betis
41 (tel: 428 0938). The usual
choice of Chinese favourites as

FOOD AND DRINK

Late-night outdoor dining is one of the delights of this city

well as authentic Chinese cheeses. Low prices for eating on the premises or *para llevar* (to take away).
Hang Zhou, Calle Mateos Gago 5 (tel: 456 0197). Popularised Chinese dishes at low prices.

Danish
Café Copenhague, Calle Vida 17 (tel: 421 0055). Efficient and pleasant place in which to enjoy Danish hot dogs and other favourites, indoors or outdoors. Ideal for a low-cost and light meal.

French
Crêperie Cibeles, Calle Betis 40 (tel: 428 2417). As the name suggests, crêpes are the speciality, but there are also other dishes of French inspiration. A simple place with low prices.

International
El 3 de Oro, Santa María de la Blanca 34 (tel: 422 27 59). A low-cost, self-service place for hungry people. Over 50 dishes, including fresh fish and meats.
Anthony's, Calle Virgen de las Montañas 2 (tel: 445 9798). Prices are relatively high, but worth it for the refined English-style décor, good service and elegant presentation of classic international dishes.
Río Grande, Betis 70 (tel: 427 39 56). Well priced for its standards, with fairly good service and average cooking of international dishes and a choice of Andaluz staples. What makes it very popular is its position, giving splendid views across the river to the Torre del Oro and the city beyond.

Italian
O'Mamma Mia, Calle Betis 33 (tel: 427 2156). Cheap and cheerful with the usual choice of pastas and pizzas.
Trastevere, Salado 6 (tel: 427 14 36). Among quite a number of Italian eateries in the city, this one has gained a good reputation for the choice and quality of its pizzas.

Jewish
Tel Aviv, Calle Virgen de la Estrella 23 (tel: 445 7633). Budget prices for *shoarmas* of meat and fish, and other favourites of Jewish cooking.

Seafood
This is just a small selection. There are many others.
El Ancora, Virgen de la Huerta, corner with Calle Paraiso (tel: 427 38 49). Prices are low for the fresh seafoods. Fish, fried or *a la sal* (baked in salt), is the

speciality.

Barca de Don Raimundo, Calle Placentines 25 (tel: 421 0334). An experienced restaurateur offers a wide variety of seafood from Andalucía's Atlantic and Mediterranean coasts in a typical setting of picturesque marine decoration. Generally, prices are moderate.

La Dorada, Virgen de Agua Santas 6 (tel: 445 51 00). Like its sister restaurants in Barcelona, Madrid and Marbella, this one is supplied daily with fresh fish from the company's own boats. The fish is prepared to perfection and stylishly served in a nautical ambience. *Frito malagueño* (a variety of crisply fried fish) and *dorada a la sal* are house specialities. Prices are reasonable for the standards and quality.

Pleamar, Calle Gustavo Bacarisas 1 (tel: 427 7980). Typically Sevillan preparation of shellfish and fish, mostly from the Atlantic, at moderate prices in a functional and efficient restaurant.

Valencian

L'Arróz, Calle Juan A Cavestany 6 (tel: 441 9103). Paellas, other rice dishes and fish, prepared in the style of Valencia, are served at appealing prices in this bright and airy place.

Vegetarian

La Mandragora, Calle Albuera 11 (tel: 441 9103). Imaginative, home-style cooking of vegetarian dishes as well as homemade desserts and liqueurs. Prices are moderate. Evening meals only Thursday to Saturday.

Dressed to kill? This embroidery graces a bullfighting costume

SHOPPING

Seville's shopkeepers prepared early for Expo'92 by increasing their prices, and prices are likely to remain high for some time. Bargains are rare, but you may find good buys in the markets. The best shopping is likely to be in things which you can only get in Seville, or for which the city offers the best choice—mainly craft items and work by local artists. If bargain hunting and careful expenditure are not priorities, Seville is a very tempting city in which to be let loose with credit or charge cards. It has glamorous shops for fashions, fashion accessories, jewellery and modern design, featuring not only local talent but also designers from around

SHOPPING

Spain and abroad. See also
Excursions for details of the
specialities of other towns and
cities.

The majority of shops are open
Monday to Saturday from 09.30
or 10.00 to 13.30 or 14.00 hrs, and
then from 16.30 or 17.00 to 19.30,
20.00 or 20.30 hrs. Some may
close on Saturday afternoons and
many do so in the summer.
Department stores do not close
for lunch.

Shopping Areas

Pedestrianised **Calle Sierpes** is
the city's principal shopping
street, and most of the streets in
close proximity, like Cuna,
Campana, O'Donnell and
Velázquez, are lined with top
fashion and accessories shops,
department stores and a variety
of speciality retailers. If time is
short this is the area on which to

Allow time for window shopping

concentrate. In the **Barrio de
Santa Cruz** there is a good
choice of art, craft and souvenir
shops. In the **Nervion** district to
the east a growing shopping
area is centred on a branch of El
Cortes Inglés department store.
Los Remedios has a full choice of
shops, serving the everyday
needs of local residents and
seekers after modern fashion.
The Cerámica Santa Ana is
enough reason to make a
shopping trip into the **Triana**
district where you will find other
craftshops, houseware and
secondhand shops worth
exploring.

Specialist Shopping

Antiques

Look in the streets east of the
cathedral, including Calles

Placentines, Mateos Gago and Rodrigo Caro. Two shops in the vicinity also worth looking into are: **Antonio Gil Martínez**, Calle Muñoz y Pabón 4; **Arcangel Antigüedades**, Calle Cabeza del Rey Don Pedro 19. To the north, near the Palacio de las Dueñas, is **El Mercadillo de Teresa**, Calle Jerónimo Hernández 6, where owner Carmen displays a fascinating collection of carefully bought pieces, useful or capricious, in six large rooms. See also **Markets** below.

Art
Calles Harinas, Zaragoza and Canalejas are good streets in which to look. Three galleries whose painting and sculpture shows are usually well received are: **Garduno**, Calle Rivero 6; **Marta Moore**, Calle Velarde 9; and **Rafael Ortiz**, Calle Mármoles 12. Two galleries presenting graphic art are **Niel-Lo**, Calle Bustos Tavera 1, and **Mama Graf**, Calle Montecarmelo 59. **Foto Foto**, Calle Luis Montoto 4, has shows of photography and sells exhibits. Under **Nightlife** see also: La Carboneria, Café Bar Tema and Café Pub Linea; and look in the local press and at billboards advertising new openings and exhibitions.

Books, Newspapers, Magazines, Music
Esteban, Calle Alemanes 15, stocks books, magazines, newspapers and is especially good for guides, city plans and road maps, as well as books about Seville and Andalucía. **Antonio Machado**, Calle Alvarez Quintero 5, has a good choice of books as well as records, cassettes and compact discs

ranging from classical to new tendencies. **Vitruvio**, Plaza de la Contración 5, specialises in books on art and architecture. **Repiso**, Calle Cerrajería 4, is a good general bookshop with a branch at Calle Acetres 1, specialising in language books and material.

Crafts
The principal local craft products are ceramics, silver and gold work, leather items including saddlery, embroidered and other textiles, decorated fans, wrought iron, guitars and castanets. It is a good idea to look around comparing quality and prices before making a purchase. See also **Markets** below.

Ceramics
Cerámica Santa Ana, San Jorge 31, has been making a wide choice since 1870. **Cerámica Sevilla**, Calle Gloria 5, is one of several places in Barrio de Santa Cruz with a wide range. **La Cartuja de Sevilla**, Carretera de Mérida, is the factory making the best known selection of local ceramics and tableware, also sold at many points within the city.

Silver and gold
Three places to start looking: **Jesús Domínguez**, Calle Santa Clara 89; **Marmolejo**, Calle Sol 7; **Triana**, Calle Pureza 66. Keep your eyes open for similar items in the main shopping streets and in markets.

Leather
Guarnicionería San Pablo, Calle Bailén, is a small workshop making various leather goods and specialising in Andalucian horse fittings. **Juan Foronda**,

Calle Argote de Molina 18, sells high quality leather and suede items. **El Caballo**, Calle Antonia Díaz 7, is a smart shop with all the gear for horseriding.

Castanets and guitars

For castanets go to **Filigrana**, Calle Cereza 3, and **Hernández**, Calle Purgatorio 6. For guitars look in at **Pantoja**, Calle Pozo 20, and at general music shops.

Embroidery, tapestries and textiles

Artesaní a Textil, Calle García de Vinuesa 35; **Bordados Artesanía**, Plaza Doña Elvira 4; **Convento Santa Isabel**, Calle Iníesta 2.

Fans

Along Calle Sierpes, **Casa Rubio**, number 56, and **Díaz**, 71, should be the first stops in a search for *abanicos* of good quality.

Wrought iron

Forja Hispalense, Calle Feria 130. Also look in department stores as well as houseware and lighting shops.

Department Stores

El Cortes Inglés, Plaza Duque de la Victoria (tel: 422 09 31), is Seville's main branch of Spain's top department store. There is another branch in the Nervion district. A bit more downmarket and lower in prices, but with similar departments and services, is **Galerías Preciados**, Plaza de la Magdalena (tel: 422 20 14).

Design, Gifts, Mementoes

Artespaña, Rodríguez Jurado 4, is a government-sponsored national chain offering design from traditional to the very latest in furnishings and other items from around Spain.

Maspapeles, Zaragoza 17, sells writing papers and all sorts of other things made from paper and board. *Expo-Info*, Plaza de Cuba 10, has articles with Expo'92 motifs—T-shirts, ceramics, folders, and so on. **Elektra Comic**, Zaragoza 10, specialises in brooches, badges, laminates and postcards; **Dibujos Animados**, Cuesta del Rosario 16, has educational and craft toys.

Drugstore

Vips, Avenida de República Argentina 23. Part of a successful national chain which stocks a wide range of 'essentials'—the sort of things you may need when all else is closed. (Vips stays open until 03.00 hrs.) There is also a pleasant cafeteria.

Fashion

American and British visitors will find that clothing of comparable quality is generally higher priced than in their home countries. It makes sense to look for things which you cannot find in your own country; and remember that El Corte Inglés department store carries wide ranges of quality fashionwear. Although the name sounds Italian, **Massimo Dutti**, Calle Tetuán 12, is a growing chain of shops for men which is very much a Spanish success story, based on good design and quality at reasonable prices. **O'Kean**, Plaza Nueva 13, has exclusive labels for classic styles and carries a selection of fine shirts. **Carmen Peral**, Muñoz Olivá 5, stocks women's fashion clothing and footwear by leading Spanish designers. **Vitorio y Luchino**, Calle Sierpes 87, are a male team designing for women, and as Seville's most successful

Awnings keep the shoppers cool

designers have contributed to Spain's quick blossoming into a world centre of designer fashions. **Adolfo Domíniquez**, Calle Rioja 1, is probably the best-known Spanish designer and designs for both men and women. **Zara**, Calle Tetuán 10, is a popular boutique with young Sevillanos of both sexes. **Loewe**, Plaza Nueva 13, is part of a much respected national chain with leatherwear and accessories.

Accessories and jewellery
Luque, Calle Cuna 14, stocks a wide choice of handbags and other leather items. **Hugo Bermond**, Calle Mateos Gago 15, has very smart leather goods. **Garach**, Calle Tetuán 14, and **Romea**, Calle Rioja 3, are just two of the many tempting shoeshops. For fragrances, pop into the quaint **Casa de las Esencias**, corner of Plaza Salvador and Calle Cuna. **Shaw**, Plaza Nueva, is a good place to start looking for jewellery. For more modern design look at shops along Calle Asunción in Los Remedios.

Local dress
Feliciano Forondo, Calle Alvarez Quintero 52, is one place to go for *mantillas*, the delicate headdresses for women. To see, and perhaps buy, *trajes de flamenca* (flamenco outfits for women) go to **Pardales**, Calle Cuna 23; **Los Azahares**, Calle Angostillo 2; or **Esperanza Flores**, Calle Asunción 68. For the local male costume, go to **Rofer**, Avenida de la Prensa 31. **Maquedano**, Calle Sierpes 40, exclusively sells sombreros; **A Garcia**, Calle Alcaicería 29, stocks these wide-brimmed traditional hats, and others.

SHOPPING

Local ceramics can be a good buy

Markets

For free entertainment and possibly some good buys, do not miss the city's bustling markets. *Mercado* means market; a *rastro* or *mercadillo* is a fleamarket.

Daily
Mercado El Postigo, near Plaza del Cabildo, business hours: a municipally sponsored craft market.

Sunday
Alameda de Hércules, until 15.00hrs: a *mercadillo* with many stalls selling antiques, bric-à-brac (old and new), crafts and much else.

Plaza del Cabildo, until 14.00hrs: coins, stamps and old postcards are sold and bought.

Plaza de la Alfalfa, until 14.00hrs: birds and other domestic pets.

Calle San Martín de Porres, in Triana, until 14.00hrs: a local *mercadillo* which has bargain

housewares and clothing.

Wednesday and Thursday
Calles Rioja and Magdalena, through the day: arts, crafts and jewellery.

Thursday
Calle Feria, '*el Jueves*', until 15.00hrs; the city's biggest fleamarket, with antiques and almost anything imaginable that is secondhand.

Friday and Saturday
Plaza del Duque de la Victoria, through the day: arts, crafts and jewellery.

Food and Drink

Local specialities are well worth investigating, for treats, gifts or souvenirs. There are numerous places to buy tempting chocolates, pastries, cakes and the like—try: **Horno San Buenaventura**, Carlos Cañal 28, and **Confitería La Campana**, Sierpes 1. For special associations with the city there are the sweet delicacies made by nuns. In the **Convento de San Leandro**, Plaza San Ildefonso, they make their unique *yemas* (egg yolk sweets) to a secret recipe. **La Casa de Los Licores**, Calle Virgen de Luján 35, and other shops have comprehensive selections of Spanish wines and local brandies, other spirits and liqueurs. Look first in supermarkets and shops in residential neighbourhoods, which usually have the best prices. **Al-Tarab Tienda Naturista**, Pasaje de los Azahares, Local 42, sells fresh and cooked natural foodstuffs and other health products, plus natural cosmetics and detergents.

ACCOMMODATION

Thanks to Expo'92, Seville has one of the best ranges of accommodation in Europe for a city of its size. Many existing places have been refurbished and modernised. New projects of good design and construction in and around the city are increasing the supply of hotel and apartment accommodation from 10,000 to 24,000 beds or 42,000 within a two-hour drive of the city. Besides these there is a well-established alternative, available for many years during Semana Santa and the Feria de Abril, of accommodation for around 50,000 people in private homes and apartment blocks, college residences, convents and camping sites. For Expo'92, travel agencies and tour operators throughout Europe should have computerised access to both regular hotel accommodation and the alternatives, arranged by the CORAL and EXHIBIT organisations respectively. During 1992, you are advised to make reservations well in advance through a travel agent or tour operator in your country. Inclusive packages of flight and accommodation are likely to be cheaper as well as easier than making independent arrangements. Package deals are also available to resorts on the Costa de la Luz and Costa del Sol, from which you can easily make day or short-stay excursions to Seville. Or you could consider a package tour of Andalucía, taking in Córdoba and Granada as well as Seville. Spain's tourist office in your country can provide lists of package operators and give basic information about officially classified places of accommodation, but it will not make reservations. Package deals may also be advertised in the press.

If you are already in Spain, local tourist offices will provide information about accommodation in Seville but again they will not make bookings. Bookings can be made through a travel agent such as Viajes Melía, a large nationwide and international group of good repute. As a rule you will do better booking on a room-only basis. Breakfast in a nearby bar will be cheaper and gives you the opportunity to start your day among local people; and you do not want to be committed to having lunch and dinner in the same place all the time when there are so many good eating places in the city. Depending on the demand generated by Expo'92, accommodation prices may seem high. In the build-up to 1992 hotel prices were the highest in Spain. This may be followed by an excess of supply over regular demand from business and vacation visitors, however, which would drive prices down.

The following is an indicative, and not exhaustive, selection of recommended hotels, *hostales* and apartments. Officially registered accommodation is available in: *Hoteles* and *Hotel apartamentos*, 1- to 5-star (5-star *Gran Lujo* is the top); *Apartamentos Turisticos*, 1- to 3-key; *Hostales*, 1- to 3-star; *Pensiones, Fondas* (Inns) and

ACCOMMODATION

Casas de Huéspedes (Guest Houses); Camping, 1- to 3-class. Prices are officially registered annually. They should be on display, and should state the rate of value-added tax (IVA). See also **Excursions** for some places to stay in other towns.

East Bank

5-star

Alfonso XIII, Calle San Fernando 2 (tel: 422 2850), *gran lujo*, 149 rooms, garage. Guests are cosseted in luxury within this mock-Mudéjar edifice, and almost every conceivable service is available. The building is leased from the municipality and the hotel is run by the French group, Ciga Hotels. The liveried staff can be somewhat over-attentive and intimidating. There is a pleasant garden and a swimming pool; the Itálica restaurant is used by monied Sevillanos and rich visitors.

The luxurious hotel Alfonso XIII

Tryp Colón, Calle Canalejas 1 (tel: 422 2900), 211 rooms, garage. Top luxury and full services are offered in a noble building. The hotel has traditionally been used by matadors and it is where many get dressed before appearing in the Maestranza ring. The El Burladero restaurant, with typically Andaluz décor, has a good reputation for its local and international dishes.

4-star

Doña María, Calle Don Remondo 19 (tel: 422 4990), 61 rooms. 'Your Palace in Seville' is a totally delightful residential hotel (which means no dining room) in the heart of the city. All the bedrooms are differently furnished with antiques, and the staff are friendly and obliging. There is a rooftop terrace, bar and swimming pool with good views. The only drawback is the regular night-time ringing of the nearby Giralda's bells. Earplugs are the solution.

Inglaterra, Plaza Nueva 7 (tel: 422 4970), 116 rooms, parking. Modern, spacious and convenient to main shopping areas, it looks across the plaza towards the Ayuntamiento. Try to get a room on the upper floors for a better view and less traffic noise.

Just behind Plaza España:

Meliá Sevilla, Calle Doctor Pedro de Castro 1 (tel: 442 2611), 366 rooms, garage. Much used by executives; has a pool.

Pasarela, Avenida de la Borbolla 11 (tel: 441 5511), 82 rooms, garage. Benefits from being small.

Further east, close to the Estadio

Sánchez Pizjuán in the Nervion district:

Porta Coeli, Avenida Eduardo Dato 49 (tel: 457 0040), 146 rooms, parking. Garden, outdoor and indoor pools.

Sol Lebreros, Calle Luis de Morales 2 (tel: 457 9400), 439 rooms, garage. The Sol Group of hotels is Spain's biggest operator and there is a similar standard and feel to all its hotels in different categories. This one is big and is often used for conventions and seminars. Garden and swimming pool. Another Sol hotel in a different part of town is:

Sol Macarena, San Juan de Ribera 2 (tel: 437 5700), 305 rooms, parking. Facing the Hospital Cinco Llagas, Murallas and Basilica Macarena, this is a good-looking, ochre-coloured building which provides full facilities for leisure and business travellers. It too has a pool.

Two new establishments of this rating due to open for 1992 in the south of the city:

Al-Andalus Palace, Avenida de la Palmera, near B Villamarín stadium, 700 rooms, garage.

Armendariz, Paseo de su Eminencia 15, 89 one-bedroom hotel apartments, parking.

3-star

Three fairly similar places in this grading are located quite close together north of Calle Campana:

América, Calle Jesús del Gran Poder 2 (tel: 422 0951), 100 rooms, garage below El Cortes Inglés store. Try for upper rooms looking on to Plaza del Duque. Very convenient for the main shopping area.

ACCOMMODATION

Corregidor, Calle Morgado 17 (or Amor de Dios 36) (tel: 438 51111), 69 rooms. Typical Andaluz construction with flower-filled patios.
Venecia, Trajano 31 (tel: 438 1161), 24 rooms. Intimate residential hotel.
Two hotels, unstylish but functional, are located on and just off Calle Reyes Católicos, near to Paseo de Cristóbal Colón and the Río Guadalquivir:
Bécquer, Calle Reyes Católicos 4 (tel: 422 8900), 126 rooms.
Reyes Católicos, Calle Gravina 51 (tel: 421 1200), 26 rooms.

2-star

Internacional, Calle Aguilas 17 (tel: 421 3207), 26 rooms, garage. Near the Casa de Pilatos and lively Plaza de Alfalfa, with the basic comforts of this grading.
Murillo, Calle Lope de Rueda 7 (tel: 421 6095), 61 rooms. Also **Apartamentos Murillo** which accommodate three or five people. These are well-managed and comfortable, in the heart of the Barrio de Santa Cruz.
La Rabida, Calle Castelar 24 (tel: 422 0960), 100 rooms. A handsome renovated building in an interesting part of the city. Old-fashioned but comfortable, with a pretty patio garden.
Sevilla, Calle Daoiz 5 (tel: 438 4161), 32 rooms. Simple residential hotel near main shopping area.

1-star

Madrid, Calle San Pedro Martir 14 (tel: 421 4306) and **Zaida**, Calle San Roque 26 (tel: 421 1138). Two small hotels of around 50 capacity each, with similar basic,

The Internacional is central

clean accommodation near the Museo de Bellas Artes.

Simon, Calle García de Vinuesa 19 (tel: 422 6660), 47 rooms. This hotel completely deserves the success it enjoys—it always seems to be full. It is extremely well located, has been tastefully renovated, is very comfortable and has friendly and helpful staff. Prices are relatively sensible for this city. The food and service in its attractive dining room are also highly recommended.

Comfortable Hotel Murillo

West Bank

5-star
Principe de Asturias, Isla de Cartuja (tel: 429 2222), *gran lujo*, 283 rooms, parking. An investment in excess of 4,000 million pesetas has been made in what will be Seville's newest 'grand luxury' hotel when it opens for 1992 with every modern facility.

4-star
Husa Sevilla, Calle Pagés del Corro 90 (tel: 434 2412), 124 rooms, garage. This hotel of the Husa chain is modern and unexceptional for its price, but certainly comfortable and functional.

3-star
Montecarmelo, Turia 9 (tel: 427 9000), 68 rooms, garage. One of the few places where visitors can get accommodation in the Los Remedios district. Similar to its sister, the Monte Triana, but its Sevillan décor is more dated. **Monte Triana**, Calle Clara de Jesús Montero 24 (tel: 434 3111), 117 rooms, garage. Simple modern design and fittings. Bedrooms are on the small side but adequate.

City Outskirts
All these are new in 1992:

5-star
Andalusi Park, Benacazon, 12 miles (20km) west along the autovía to Huelva (tel: 570 5499), 206 rooms.

4-star
Alcora, San Juan de Aznalfarache, just southwest of the city on the autovía to Coria del Río (tel: 429 0092).

3-star
La Motilla, Urbanización La Motilla, 5 miles (8km) south on the autovía to Cádiz, 198 rooms.

3-key
Apartamentos Mairena, Mairena del Aljarafe, 4 miles (6.5km) southwest, 40 studio apartments. **Apartamentos El Olivar**, Urbanización La Motilla, 5 miles (8km) south on the autovía to Cádiz.

CULTURE, ENTERTAINMENT AND NIGHTLIFE

Although it has always had a little of everything, from the most sophisticated to the very seedy, Seville's nightlife has traditionally been relatively subdued, except during its fiestas. But this is changing, thanks to Expo'92 and expectations of many more visitors, in the long term as well as the short. Many new venues for cultural and leisure pursuits are opening throughout the city, including superb venues like the Teatro and the Auditorio on the Expo'92 site. Together with the new Teatro de Maestranza and the Teatro Lope de Vega, they will be settings for a greatly increased number of opera and other theatrical and musical performances. There are plans to mount large scale open-air performances in the Plaza de España and Maestranza bullring. It is a memorable experience to go to an opera in the city which forms the setting of *Carmen*, *Don Giovanni* and other operatic greats. Most music and theatre performances start at 21.00 hrs. An informal evening's entertainment should start at around 20.00 hrs, when tapas bars, cafés and cocktail bars start filling. From early spring to late autumn their customers spill out into streets and squares, like Plaza Salvador and Plaza Santa Cruz. After doing *el tapeo* (touring tapas bars) at a few traditional places, you could move on before or after dinner to a trendsetting bar like La Carboneria, to view art, hear music or see an intimate theatre

show. Or you could take in a late-night jazz session at El Sol, see a flamenco *tablao* (performance), or linger over the view of the Giralda from the terrace of the Hotel Doña María. For late night entertainment, move on to one of the music bars in Los Remedios or end the night in a disco.

Opera, Concerts, Dance, Theatre

In addition to checking what is on at the venues listed below, look in the media and on billboards to see if there are concerts in churches or open-air events.

Teatro Lope de Vega, Avenida María Luisa. The theatre and the Casino de la Exposición were built for the Ibero-América exhibition of 1929. Under the auspices of the Ayuntamiento de Sevilla, it has since then been the city's principal venue for theatre and music.

Teatro de la Maestranza, Paseo de Cristóbal Colón. National, regional, provincial and municipal authorities, as well as Expo'92, sponsored the building of the new Palacio de Cultura. The design by Rafael Moneo, which incorporates the old façade of the Maestranza Artillería, has not been without its critics, but Seville can now boast of having the largest theatre stage in Europe, with the very latest technical equipment and modern comfort for an audience up to 1,800. It will be the city's principal venue for opera and classical concerts.

Teatro Central, Isla de la Cartuja. This is Spain's first venue designed for and dedicated to alternative theatre, and it will also be used for performances of avant garde dance. Architect

Gerardo Ayala has designed the large hall with a square stage and movable modular seating, so that audience capacity can vary from 500 to 1,000.

Auditorio Cartuja, Isla de la Cartuja. The exceptionally large stage makes possible the presence of the world's great ballet companies with their complete casts. Most forms of top-rated musical performances will be presented here, from light opera through flamenco, jazz and soul to pop and rock.

Auditorio Municipal, Prado de San Sebastián. The main municipal venue for musical concerts, from classical to pop and rock.

Teatro Imperial, Calle Sierpes. The Centro Andaluz de Teatro (CAT) is based here. A knowledge of Spanish is usually necessary for the full enjoyment of its performances.

Teatro Alameda, Calle Calatrava. This is another municipally sponsored venue which presents a varied programme of theatre.

Laimperdible, Plaza San Antonio de Padua 9. Both the Junta de Andalucía and Ayuntamiento de Sevilla give support to this venue for avant garde theatre.

Teatro Lope de Vega

CULTURE, ENTERTAINMENT AND NIGHTLIFE

Paraninfo de la Universidad, Calle San Fernando. The university's venue for different cultural presentations which are open to the public.
Conservatorio Superior de Musica, Calle Jesús del Gran Poder. Concerts by famous or still-unknown soloists, ensembles and choirs, or by the city's orchestra, Bética Flarmónica de Sevilla.

Flamenco and Sevillanas

You cannot have a complete experience of Seville without seeing a performance of flamenco. If you are lucky you will witness a spontaneous outburst of authentic, emotional

Fiery flamenco at Los Gallos

flamenco in a street, plaza or bar, which will probably leave a deeper impression than one of the commercial *tablaos*. These shows have to a greater or lesser extent diluted their authenticity in popularising the performances for undiscerning tourists' tastes. That said, you will be missing out if you do not go to one of them. Tickets can be bought from hotels or you can make your own reservations. They are usually open from 21.00hrs to the early morning.

El Patio Sevillano, Paseo de Cristóbal Colón 11 (tel: 421 41 20). The programme also includes performances of Spanish songs and the classical guitar. Respected by *aficionados* (informed enthusiasts).

Arenal, Calle Rodo 7 (tel: 421 64 92). Here too there will be both knowledgeable *aficionados* and enthralled foreigners.

Los Gallos, Plaza de Santa Cruz (tel: 421 69 81). This is a stylish venue where you will hear more of the *cante jondo*—the 'deep song' that is the most haunting expression of flamenco.

Sevillanas
If you want to see or join in the graceful dances called *sevillanas*, go after 22.00hrs to the **Taberna Flamenca Puerto de Triana**, Calle Castilla 137. It has become one of 'the' places in the city to show off an ability in the dance form which has become so popular throughout Spain.

Jazz
See Auditorio Cartuja and Auditorio Municipal above. If you think jazz is not genuine unless the venue is slightly seedy, go to **El Sol**, Sol 40, for its late night sessions. **El Patio**, Calle San Laureano 2 (corner of Calles Alfonso XII and Torneo), also has a variety of local and imported live jazz.

Rock and Pop
The Auditorio Cartuja and Auditorio Municipal are venues for big concerts, and there are many places with live performances by local and visiting bands. Check in the local press, on billboards and give-away leaflets. **Fun Club**, Alameda de Hércules 86, often has good live rock music as well as art exhibitions and avant garde theatre.

Cafés, Bars, Discos
Ask modern Sevillano mainstreamers how they enjoy themselves at night and the answer is likely to be that they go to a bar, stroll in the *calles* and *plazas*, have a few drinks, listen to music, meet friends and talk a lot. Discos are not part of the scene in Seville, except perhaps 'for the kids'. The following are just a few of the places where you will find Sevillanos at leisure in the evening and through the night. At the heart of the city, close to the cathedral and Giralda, **Placentines**, Placentines 2, is a long-time favourite for its nostalgic ambience, and for the performances on classical guitar which often take place at around 23.00hrs. The **Terraza de Hotel Doña María**, Calle Don Remondo, has a pool and bar and is one of the best places from which to get a memorable view of the floodlit Giralda. The trendsetting **La Carboneria**, Leviás 18, should be an essential

stop on a nocturnal itinerary. It is attractive and friendly, has art exhibitions, presents a variety of music and often features theatre shows.
Abades, Abades 13, is a delightfully altered old town house: dress well, join a stylish crowd and listen to quiet classical music in the select atmosphere of the rooms and patio. There is usually louder and heavier music in the **Café Sevilla**, Miguel de Mañara 9, which stays open 24 hours and where many all-night revellers come for reviving coffee and a light breakfast. **La Catedral**, Cuesta del Rosario, where the doorman has to like your looks, was, at the time of going to press, the disco in Seville where it was most socially advantageous to be seen, for those to whom it mattered.
With the coming of spring, the **Plaza Salvador** begins filling each evening with an animated crowd of all ages which spills out across it from the bar in the southwest corner on to the steps of the church opposite. In the nearby Alfalfa area, **Bar Alcaicería**, corner of Calles Alcaicería and Empecinado, is one of several lively bars. **Bar Europa**, corner of Calles Alcaicería and Siete Revueltos, has aimed to recreate *el sabor del viejo Europa*, the flavour of old Europe, and it has largely succeeded. Also close by, **Sopa de Ganso**, Calle Pérez Gáldos, hums with lively conversation among friends as dusk turns to dark.
A bit to the northwest are two café bars which are also art galleries: **Café Pub Linea**, Calle

Trajano 38, and **Café Bar Tema**, Calle Amor de Dios/Pasaje de Trajano. And near by, **Pub Ibio** (Antiguo Cafetín Ojalá), Plaza de Europa 9, is an old-style café where live music performances range from classical guitar through blues to rock and pop.
If you intend making your nightscene in the Triana district, doing *el tapeo* and then eating in one of its restaurants or along Calle Betis (see **Food and Drink**), you could linger a while in **Druida**, Rodrigo de Triana 96, where the décor, clientele and music are all interestingly mixed. After 01.00hrs you may want to go on to **Rrio**, Calle Betis 67, a big disco popular with the younger set.
In Los Remedios district, where there is a concentration of modern music bars, **Calle Montecarmelo** is a good street in which to start looking for a favourite: try **La Tasca**, at number 5, **Arlekin**, number 8, or **Strawberry Hill**, number 12.

Sex and Shows
Visitors are well advised to avoid any sex-for-sale situations and propositions. The robbery and health risks are high and the pain may be greater than the pleasure. The main red light area is east of Alameda de Hércules. **Florida Show**, Calle Menéndez y Pelayo 42 and **Escala's**, Calle Asunción 76, are two venues with 'sexy shows'.
Pub Arte, Calle Trastamara 19, has a refined gay ambience and nearby **Club 27**, at number 27, is a gay video-pub. Everything happens at another gay venue in the area, **Tibu's**, Calle Luis de Vargas 4.

WEATHER AND WHEN TO GO

WEATHER AND WHEN TO GO

Shopping on the Calle Sierpes . . .

Seville is a sunshine city, enjoying an average of 2,900 hours of sun a year. The low annual rainfall comes in autumn and spring. A basically Mediterranean climate is influenced by the city's proximity to the Atlantic, its inland location and mountains not far to the north and south. Average summer temperatures are around 98° Fahrenheit (37° Centigrade) and often peak uncomfortably higher at 112° Fahrenheit (45° Centigrade). Some restaurants and other businesses close during August. Winter temperatures range between a lower level of 52° Fahrenheit (11° Centigrade) and a maximum of 57° Fahrenheit (14° Centigrade), seldom dropping more than a few points below the lower figure. Spring and autumn are the ideal seasons during which to be in the city, with average temperatures around 77° Fahrenheit (25° Centigrade).

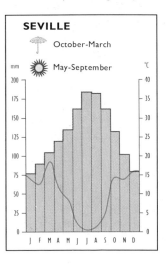

HOW TO BE A LOCAL

Through many centuries the people of southern Iberia have, while changing them, absorbed some character traits and customs of others, including conquerors and settlers from

... or try shopping like a local

Castile and northern parts of Spain. A deep influence on individual and communal behaviour has been left by 536 years of Arab rule in Seville. With wider education, industrialisation, increasing wealth filtering through the social scale and mass communication, Sevillanos are

becoming more Western, and the world attention focused on them because of Expo'92 is accelerating the trend.

Seville still has sharp social contrasts and there are many different types of local. At the pinnacle there are the aristocrats whose ancestors gained their titles and wealth long ago, and who hold cultural events and grand parties in their palaces. Then there are the new rich who dress fashionably, have expensive cars and are well versed in talk about money and material things. Next there is a questing mass on the ladder of upward social movement, among whom there are many whose memory of poverty is fresh. Their concerns are to be one point up on their neighbour, to find better accommodation, to manage their bank loans and to improve the education and circumstances of their children. Still not at the foot of the ladder, there is a large section of society with many illiterate and uneducated people. Among some their poverty and hopelessness generates a life of crime and drug abuse. And then, quite separate and immune to integration, there are the gypsies. From among all these groups, sparks of artistic talent of all sorts flare out and for these people class distinction matters little.

What individual Andalucians will think about their region and people will depend on where they come from, what province, what pueblo, what barrio. A perspective of life and the world is formed within the family, still very much a matriarchal unit in which the mother is both the most revered and the most hardworked. Next in influence is the perception of the community, which can be very different in isolated pueblos, city barrios or tourist resorts. Then there is the closed circle of friends in which an Andaluz also finds solidarity and comfort. These three mingled influences protect a person but their strength can also strangle fresh thought and progress. Foreigners in search of acceptance by an Andaluz must somehow gain acceptance within one sphere of influence and then wiggle their way into the others, by acceptable behaviour and using *enchufes* (introductions), the Andaluz means of social and career progress.

It is meaningless to generalise about all Sevillans, let alone all Andalucians, but some hints on attitudes and behaviour may be helpful. Be prepared to be perplexed. Forget all preconceptions about Andalucians, especially the one that they are lazy. Be dismissive of time constraints and do not get angry when everything closes during the siesta, or on a local fiesta day, or if the person with whom you have an appointment is not there on time.

Do not object to noise but add to it and be demonstrative of emotion. Enthusiastically join in the *juerga* by living life to the full and for the moment, spending your few savings, not caring about tomorrow. Try to become known as *un listo*, 'clever one', by waxing into verse, bursting into song, or making music (and outsmarting the authorities).

CHILDREN

Laugh at jokes about death and make your own humour black and fatalistic.

Remember that the collective sanction or praise of the community is usually more meaningful than the sanction of authorities and any outside recognition. Join intercommunity rivalry by being as rude as you like about the next barrio, pueblo, town, or province. But praise the place where you are and its province, and always Andalucía as a whole. Avoid discussion about local politics and personalities, no matter how disparaging the company you are in may be about them.

Admire a man's virility and a woman's fertility; the dress and deportment of both; a woman's housekeeping and cooking skills (activities in which macho men do not engage themselves). Praise an Andaluz's mother, children and prize animals, but do not overdo the praise of an Andaluz man's wife. If you praise her husband too much, a wife will view you sceptically, for she is wise to his foibles.

Above all, be open-minded and remember you are in a society that is modernising and changing at a rapid pace.

CHILDREN

Children are made to feel very welcome and they usually get more attention than their parents from Andalucians, who, like most Mediterranean people, tend to idolise the young. Local children stay up late, often having a siesta to compensate, and it is not unusual to see them dropping off to sleep in a neighbourhood

restaurant well after midnight, while the conversation and merrymaking of the adults goes on unabated. In Seville there are numerous playparks, for example in the Parque de María Luisa, as well as *guardecas* (daytime care centres) and babysitting services.

Information and advice about these are best sought from local tourist offices. They can also advise about any special events for children. Some fiestas and ferias have diversions for children.

That said, the main attractions of Seville are not ideal for all children. Parents have found that their time in the city has been

On the steps of Plaza de España

TIGHT BUDGET

more enjoyable and rewarding without having children in tow. However, Expo'92 is changing the situation, both as an exciting and memorable experience for children, with strong educational elements, and in the long term—the Expo site on La Cartuja island will have a number of museums, exhibitions and other amenities of interest to children. See also **Excursions**, for instance to the beaches of the Costa de la Luz, Cuevas de Maravillas (Aracena) and Palos de la Frontera, from where Columbus first sailed to the Americas.

Investigate what budget holiday packages to Seville, or tours of Andalucía including a stay in Seville, are available from your country. These often work out far cheaper than arranging travel and accommodation independently. They may also give you access to events for which it could be difficult to obtain tickets yourself. If you are organising your own travel arrangements, ask travel agents specialising in budget travel about lower-cost charter flights (especially to Málaga), special rail fares and coach travel. If you are looking for low-cost

TIGHT BUDGET

accommodation on the spot, a good central area for budget pensions is north of Calles Reyes Católicos and San Pablo, in streets like Gravina and Bailén. Budget accommodation in the delightful Barrio de Santa Cruz is more at a premium. Across the river, there is limited but even cheaper accommodation in the Triana district. You can stay relatively cheaply in other parts of the city, but there will be more trudging around finding a place you like and inspecting the rooms on offer. There are budget eating places in all parts of the city, getting cheaper as you move away from the centre into residential neighbourhoods. Bear in mind though: all businesses, even the humblest, are seeking a financial bonanza out of Expo '92 and perhaps its aftermath.

● Avoid places which display an array of credit card signs.

● Ordering a choice of tapas or raciones can work out more costly than taking the *menú del día*.

● Beer is cheaper if you ask for *una caña* (draught), and a *vino*

Helping to feed the white doves in the Plaza de América

de la casa (house wine) will be lower priced.

- Buying food and drink in a market or shop to make up a meal for enjoying outdoors—in a plaza, along the river or in the Parque de María Luisa—is a cost-saving alternative.
- A small supply of food and drink in your room is another saving standby, but avoid turning your room into a kitchen.
- Walking is not only the cheapest way of getting around the city, it is also the best way to get to know it. Get acquainted with and use the city bus network.
- For excursions from Seville, use local buses or trains, or make up a party with like-minded people to rent a car or minibus.
- For entertainment, taking an evening *paseo* (stroll) and indulging in people-watching is a cheap option.
- If you want to visit a fashionable gathering place, make the most of the cost by lingering over your drink (the locals do).
- Search out places where students and other young people gather, like Plazas Salvador and Alfalfa.
- For details of free entertainment, check the local press, look at billboards as well as notices in café bars, enquire at tourist offices and ask at the Ayuntamiento's Area de Cultura, Calle General Moscardó 1.
- For budget shopping, avoid the central shopping district and Barrio de Santa Cruz and look in residential neighbourhoods like Triana. The same applies to shopping in other towns.

SPECIAL EVENTS

On 6 January in the **Labalyata de los Reyes**, the Three Kings parade on floats throwing sweets to bystanders.

Lent is preceded by the extravagant consumption and colourful merrymaking of **Carnival** which closes on Ash Wednesday (February/March). Groups and bands called *chirigotas* and *comparsas* perform songs laden with irony. The Carnival of Cádiz is among the most flamboyant in Europe. From February into March, the **Ancient Music Festival** features original or replica instruments in performances.

Seville mounts Spain's most spectacular celebration of **Semana Santa** (Holy Week—March/April) in a display of religious devotion verging on the pagan in its ritual and zeal. From Palm Sunday to Easter Sunday the processions of some 60 *cofradías* (brotherhoods) pace slowly through dark and ominously quiet streets with their elaborately carved and decorated *pasos* (floats) on which revered images of Christ and the Virgin are borne. *Costaleros*, members of the brotherhoods as well as paid bearers, sweat under the heavy burden. In the procession are hundreds of berobed and hooded *nazarenos*, who would once have been serious penitents. Muffled drums beat sonorously and zealous bystanders, or professional singers, call out haunting *saetas* in devotion and praise of the images. The smell of incense

Sevillanos of all ages get dressed up for the feria

and candlewax hangs heavily in the air. The deepest passions are reserved for late on Thursday night through to the dawn of Good Friday, when the pasos of the city's most revered images, *La Macarena* and *Jesús del Gran Poder*, leave their churches at 24.00 and 02.00 hrs respectively.

Unless it coincides with Easter, the week-long **Feria de Abril** starts on 18 April. What began as a livestock fair last century is now among the world's most colourful celebrations of spring. It is a high-society parade and a time for showing off by the rich and influential—groups of people, businesses, organisations and government bodies. It is also a time for having the right invitations and connections if you want to be at the heart of the celebrations; but even without these other Sevillanos and visitors still have great fun during the feria. Some of the many *casetas* in the huge fairground are open to the public, and inside these temporary constructions the wine flows freely, food is abundant, and the music and dancing go on until the early hours. Each day Spain's top matadors kill 12 bulls in the Maestranza ring. Another highlight is the *paseo de caballos* when men and women in their finest Andaluz dress parade on horseback or in fine carriages. Accommodation must be booked many months in advance, everybody puts up their prices, few people work at their usual jobs, streets are closed to traffic, and people have very little interest in anything else but the feria and their enjoyment of it.

Also at this time of year, Seville's **Antiques Fair** is regarded by many as Spain's best, and has exhibitors from all parts of the country.

Cruces de Mayo at the beginning of May sees the placing in neighbourhood plazas of crosses decorated with paper flowers, and children repeating the Easter processions with pasos of wood and cardboard.

Cita de Sevilla runs through into June with its varied cultural programme of high-standard live performances in almost all forms of expression, as well as exhibitions of various kinds.

El Rocío is Spain's largest *romería* (pilgrimage to a shrine). On the Wednesday before Whitsun over a million pilgrims, on horseback, in brightly decorated carts and carriages, in cars or on foot, start from the Iglesia de San Salvador, the Triana district and other points to

make their way to the tiny hamlet of El Rocío in Huelva province. After merrymaking on the way, they arrive on the Saturday and that night the image of the Virgin, *La Blanca Paloma*, is paraded among the massed crowds and competing *cofradías* in a frenzy of excitement verging on hysteria. **Corpus Christi** (sometimes in June) is marked by a big procession through streets strewn with rose petals, sedge and rosemary, past balconies decorated with palm leaves and flowers. Choirboys, *los seises*, in fine costumes, do 14th-century dances in the cathedral. **Corpus Chico**, Triana's smaller procession is the following day.

Top international theatre and dance companies perform in the Roman amphitheatre during the **Itálica Festival** in July. In the same month, neighbourhoods have fun in their *voladas*—mini ferias—of which that of Triana at the end of the month is the biggest and liveliest. September in even-numbered years sees the **Bienal de Flamenco**, with the best of Andalucía's and Spain's flamenco guitarists, dancers and singers performing the region's music. The November **international jazz festival** presents top Spanish and international musicians. On 8 December the city is again deep in devotion, this time for **La Immaculada**, the Immaculate Conception, especially venerated in the city since Seville was at the forefront of defending the belief during the 17th century. The dogma is portrayed in much of Seville's religious art.

SPORT

Iglesia Jesús del Gran Poder

SPORT

Sevillanos are not known for any great enthusiasm for participant sports and their city attracts few visitors intent on spending their time practising their favourite sport. Most facilities are offered by clubs with membership requirements. If you want a sports-filled holiday in Andalucía, head for the many excellent facilities of the Costa del Sol or the growing number on the Costa de la Luz. Tarifa, Europe's most southerly point in Cádiz province, is a sailboarding mecca and venue for international competitions, and there is the winter sports resort of Solynieve in Granada province, 1995 venue for the World Skiing Championships. The municipal **Palacio de los Deportes**, Avenida de Kansas City, has comprehensive facilities, including swimming pools, open to the public.

Club Pineda, Avenida de Jerez (tel: 461 1400), is the top social and sports club for a golf and horsey set. It includes a horseracing course and golf course among its good facilities.

Hípica Puerta Príncipa, Carretera Sevilla-Utera (tel: 486 08 15), also offers horseriding and instruction.

Las Minas Golf, Carretera Isla Mayor (tel: 475 0571), is the other local golf club. Remember: you must have your membership card from your own club.

Club Antares, Calle Antonio Maura (tel: 462 14 11), offers tennis and squash courts, and health and relaxation programmes.

Club Náutico de Sevilla, Avenida Tablada (tel: 445 47 77), is the top among a number of clubs for sailing and rowing, and organises national events.

Spectator Sports

Seville has two top league soccer clubs and *futbol* is the main spectator sport. The main teams are **Real Betis Balompié** (Benito Villamarin stadium), and **Sevilla Futbol Club** (Sanchez Pizjuan stadium). Expo'92 has provided the city with a new installation for competitive rowing and with a new athletics track for international events. Cádiz hosts the Spanish Motorcycle Championship in May and Spanish Grand Prix in September.

DIRECTORY

Arriving

Entry formalities

You require a valid passport to enter Spain. Nationals of European Community countries and some others do not need a visa for stays of up to 90 days. It is always wise to check the current situation with a Spanish tourist office or Spanish Consulate in your country. Visitors from most countries do not require any medical documents but, if in any doubt, check at one of the above places.

... and departing

left in sight, may be a temptation for a break-in); avoid lonely, seedy and dark areas; use taxis late at night; be and look aware.

Customs Regulations

Personal effects can usually be taken into Spain without payment of duty. Small amounts of wine, spirits and tobacco (up to 200 cigarettes) are also free of duty. You may have to pay a deposit against duty and taxes on valuable items such as video cassette recorders. Remember that alcohol in particular is cheaper in Spain than in many other countries.

Avenida de la Constitución

Disabled Travellers

Newer buildings are likely to have amenities such as ramps, wider doorways, and toilets. Special needs should be stated and full enquiries made before making final reservations. For general information send a stamped addressed envelope to RADAR, 25 Mortimer Street, London W1 (tel: (071) 637 5400).

Driving

Breakdown

Special arrangements may be provided by an insurance policy bought from your motoring organisation. In the case of rental vehicles, contact the rental company. Breakdown vehicles

are called *gruas*. A day and night *grua y taller* (workshop) service is available from Calle C 18, Poligono Surtele (tel: 464 36 00).

The Real Automovil Club de España, Avenida Eduardo Dato 22 (tel: 463 13 50) can provide advice.

Car rental

The big international firms operate in Seville and you can make bookings with them in your home country. Holiday operators have car rental schemes, and airlines offer 'fly-drive' deals. Renting from a smaller local firm is usually cheaper.

Documents

Licences issued by European Community countries are acceptable (for UK and Republic of Ireland drivers, licences should be of the pink EC-type). Visitors from other countries should have an international driving licence, which should be obtainable from the motoring organisations in their home country. See also **Road Signs and Rules**, below.

Fuel

The types are: normal (92 octane); super (96 octane); gas-oil (diesel); and *sin plumo* (lead-free), increasingly available.

Parking

Finding legal parking within the city can be very difficult. Carparks are the best places to leave your car and they are not expensive—but they are few. Streetside spaces are indicated by blue road and kerb markings, and tickets are bought from machines on the pavement.

Road signs and rules

Generally these are in line with those of other European countries, with eccentricities which are only comprehensible after exposure to them. The most important one is the need for a Bail Bond, otherwise you could be arrested if involved in an accident. Spain's Ministry of Transport publishes a small leaflet of advice for drivers. Try to get one at frontier posts or tourist offices. If you are driving to Spain, take advice and get information from a motoring organisation in your country, and buy appropriate insurance.

Electricity

220/230 volts AC and 110/120 in some bathrooms and older buildings. Plugs have two round pins.

Emergency Telephone Numbers

Policia Nacional	091
Policia Local	092

These 24-hour numbers will not necessarily connect you with the nearest station but will get your message relayed. Try to clearly state the nature of *urgencia* (emergency), your location and the services required.

Bomberos (Fire)	442 00 80
Cruz Roja (Red Cross)	435 12 42
Ambulances	433 09 93
First Aid	438 24 61
Emergencies	435 01 36

Entertainment Information

Daily newspapers, the free monthly *El Giraldillo* and the monthly *Revista del Ocio* provide listings. Look at billboards and pick up leaflets and information from tourist offices.

Entry Formalities see Arriving

DIRECTORY

Health

Residents of European Community countries are entitled to medical treatment from the Spanish health service, if they produce form E110, E111 or E112 (obtain this before departure). But the best advice for all foreign visitors to Spain is to buy a travel insurance policy from a reputable company which provides comprehensive cover in case of accident and illness. It is also wise to carry a photocopy of prescriptions for any medication which you are taking. Health problems are most likely to arise from over-indulgence in drink and food by people in a holiday mood. In summer, they may be due to too much sun and eating mayonnaise or 'sad' salads and *tapas*; or they may be a reaction to unfamiliar tap water (so stick to bottled water).

First Aid Casa de Socorro, Jesús del Gran Poder 34 (tel: 438 2461). There are a number of hospitals with *urgencia* departments. The teaching hospital of the university's faculty of medicine is the Hospital Universitario Macarena, Calle Doctor Fedriani (tel: 437 8400)

Holidays

Besides the variable dates of Easter and Whitsun, the principal holidays are:

Año Nuevo: 1 January
Día de los Reyes: 6 January
Día de Andalucía: 28 February
San José: 19 March
Día del Trabajo: 1 May
San Fernando: 30 May
San Juan: 24 June
Santiago: 25 July
Asunción: 15 August

Hispanidad: 12 October
Todos los Santos: 1 November
Immaculada Concepción: 8 December
Navidad: 25 December

Lost Property

There are two *Oficinas de Objetos Perdidos*: first try at Calle Almansa 23 (tel: 421 50 64) and if your lost items are not there also check with the Policia Local at Avenida de la Palmera (tel: 461 54 50) (*open*: Monday to Friday 09.30–13.30 hrs). Advise your consulate about any loss of personal documents and if necessary contact credit card companies.

Media

Periodicos (Newspapers)

Many newspapers from other European countries are available by the afternoon. International editions are on sale in the morning. The liberal national daily *El Pais* has the widest respect internationally, and publishes a Seville edition; so do other national dailies like the conservative *ABC* and the middleground *Diario 16*. *El Correo de Andalucía*, founded in 1899, and *El Sol de Andalucía* are especially strong on coverage of the region.

Revistas (Magazines)

Spain publishes a plethora of magazines. The weekly *Cambio 16* is a respected news magazine in the *Times/Newsweek* format. For sensationalism and scandal *Holai* is the leader. Among a number of foreign language magazines published on Andalucía's Costa del Sol *Lookout* (English), *Aktuelle* (German), and *Solkysten*

(Scandinavian) have articles on Spanish affairs and places.

Television
Two channels, *TVE-1* and *TVE-2*, are national and state-run. *Canal Sur* is sponsored by the Junta de Andalucía; *Tele-5*, *A-3TV* and *Canal Plus* (subscription) are private stations.

Radio
Foreign, national, regional, local—public and private—stations vie for space among the airwaves. English language stations include the BBC World Service on 15070 khz all through the day and at night until 23.30 hrs.

Money Matters

Banks
Banks are everywhere. Savings banks, mostly also offering exchange facilities, are called *cajas* (*open*: Monday to Friday 08.30–14.00 hrs; Saturday (except June to September) 08.30–13.00 hrs)—note that this means banks are generally closed on Saturdays in summer). Money exchange facilities are available outside these hours at the airport. Cashpoints issuing money around the clock with use of a credit card and PIN are plentiful.

Credit Cards
The major credit, charge and direct debit cards are widely accepted. Make a note of your credit card numbers and emergency telephone numbers to contact in case of loss, and keep it with your passport. Tell the company immediately if one of your cards is stolen or lost.

Larger banks open in the afternoon

Currency
The *peseta* is available in the following denominations: notes—10,000, 5,000, 2,000, 1,000; coins—500, 200, 100, 50, 25, 10, 5 and 1.

Tax
IVA, a value-added tax, is currently applied at 6 per cent on most goods and services and at 12 or 33 per cent on luxury items and some services. (The 12 per cent rate may rise to 14.) People resident outside Spain can gain exemption from tax on large individual purchases, but may pay tax on importation into their home country.

Opening Times

See also under **Shopping, Money Matters** and **Post Office**.
Business offices work from Monday to Friday, and general hours are 09.00–14.00 and 16.00–18.00 hrs. In the summer many businesses work *horas intensivas*, 08.00–15.00 hrs. Official organisations are generally open Monday to Friday 09.00–14.00 hrs.

Rich interior of the vast cathedral

Pharmacies

As well as selling prescription medicines, *farmacias* will provide free advice about minor injuries or ailments and suggest a non-prescription treatment from their stocks. They are easily identified by a big green or red cross sign and follow normal shopping hours. During other times they will display a sign indicating the nearest *farmacia de guardia*, which will be open. Local papers also list these.

Places of Worship

Nearly all the churches are Catholic with services in Spanish. In a few churches Catholic masses are also said in other languages at specified times. Tourist offices and consulates will provide information on places and times of worship of other Christian denominations and faiths with local communities.

Police

Officers of the three police organisations have different, sometimes confusingly overlapping roles.

Policia Local

The municipal police are mainly responsible for traffic. They have blue uniforms and white checked bands on their vehicles and caps.

Policia National

Spain's national police, also in blue, are responsible for law and order and internal security. It is to their *comisaria* that you should go to report a crime or loss and make a *denuncia* (statement). The main *comisaris* is at Plaza de la Concordia (tel: 422 8840).

Guardia Civil

Officers in olive green uniforms are mostly seen at border posts, in country areas and along the coastline. A branch of the organisation is responsible for highway patrols.

Post Office

The main *Correos* is at Avenida de la Constitución 32 (*open*: Monday to Friday 09.00–20.00 hrs, Saturday 09.00–14.00 hrs). Parcels must be collected from the *paquetería*, Avenida Molini (*open*: Monday

to Saturday 09.00–13.00 hrs). Mail can be sent addressed to you at Lista de Correos, Avenida de la Constitución, SEVILLA, España. Take personal identification when collecting. Post boxes are yellow and some have different sections for different destinations. *Sellos* (stamps) can also be bought at *estancos* (tobacconists).

Public Transport

Air

Travel agents are the best source of information, at no extra cost to the traveller. The main office of Iberia is at Calle Almirante Lobo 1. For information and reservations, tel: 421 8800.

Bus

Tussam operates the city's bus network. It is handy to have a copy of its *Plano de Red Lineas*, obtainable from tourist offices. Routes are also displayed at bus stops. Many routes run through Plaza Nueva. Single journey fares are bought on the bus. *Bonobus* saver tickets for 10 trips can be bought from *estancos* (tobacconists).

Taxis

Seville's licensed taxis are either black or white with a yellow stripe. They show a green light and *libre* sign when available for hire and can be flagged down in the street. Standard rates are shown on the meter and there are supplements for baggage or for trips at night, and for those departing from railway stations and the airport.

Trains

Details can be obtained from

travel agents and from Renfe, tel: 441 4111. Renfe's office in Seville is at Zaragoza 29; for reservations, call 442 15 62.

Senior Citizens
Check with travel agents what special package holidays in Seville or tours through Andalucía, including Seville, are available for senior citizens from your country. In the winter months, there are low-cost, long-stay holidays for senior citizens on the Costa del Sol, from which Seville is easily accessible.

Student and Youth Travel
Surprisingly, considering the number of youthful visitors Seville attracts, special facilities and programmes are limited. Consult with specialist travel agencies, tour operators and youth organisations in your own country. See also **Tight Budget**.

Telephones
The code for seven-digit numbers in Seville (city and province) is 95 and is used for calls from other provinces. To call a Seville number from outside Spain dial the international services code applicable in your country, then 34 (Spain), 5 (Seville) and the seven digit number.
International access codes are as follows. To call Spain from Australia, dial 0011; Canada 011; New Zealand 00; UK 010; US 011. Public phone booths are plentiful. They take 100, 25 and 5 peseta coins and some accept credit cards. Instructions for use are displayed in a number of languages, as are provincial and international dialling codes. Many bars also have telephones

for use by customers. To make direct international calls put at least 200 pesetas in the groove at the top (or in the slot of some telephones), dial 07 and wait for a changed tone, then dial country code, town code (without initial 0) and number. Country codes are: Australia 61; Canada 1; New Zealand 64; UK 44; US 1. You can get assistance, make reversed charge calls and pay after your call at the Telefónica *locutorio*, Plaza de la Gavidia (*open*: 10.00–14.00 and 17.30–22.00 hrs). A cheap rate applies Monday to Friday 22.00–08.00 hrs and from 20.00 hrs Saturday to 08.00 hrs Monday.

Telefax, Telex and Telegrams
Many hotels provide all of these services, but may charge double or more the cost.
Business bureaux offer telefax and (some) telex services. The telegram office is at the *Correos* (post office). For telegrams by telephone—a 24-hour service —dial 422 20 00 for services within Spain; 422 6860 for services abroad.

Time
Like most of Europe, Spain is two hours ahead of GMT (Greenwich Mean Time) in the summer and one hour ahead in the winter.

Tipping
Although most hotel and restaurant bills will include a service charge, you may still want to give a tip of between five and 10 per cent in restaurants and for special services in hotels. At bars leave less than five per cent from whatever change you get. The same

See the sights from 'un carruaje'

applies to taxis. Other people who usually get tips are carpark attendants, doormen, hairdressers, lavatory attendants and tour guides.

Toilets

Public lavatories are few and far between. There are toilet facilities at department stores, some museums and places of interest. Bars and restaurants have facilities for customers.

Tourist Offices

Turespaña of Spain's Ministry of Tourism operates offices in:
Australia: 203 Castlereagh Street, Suite 21, Sydney NSW 2000.
Canada: 102 Bloor Street West, 14th Floor, Toronto.
UK: 57–8 St James Street, London SW1A 1LD
US: 665 Fifth Avenue, New York 10022; 8383 Wilshire Bvd, Suite 960, Beverley Hills, California 90211.

DIRECTORY

In and Around Seville

Oficina Municipal de Turismo,
Costurero de la Reina, Paseo de
las Delicias 9 (tel: 423 44 65);
Oficina de Turismo (Junta de
Andalucía), Avenida de la
Constitución 21B (tel: 422 14 04);
Aeropuerto de San Pablo (tel:
425 50 46).

Antequera: Palacio de Nájera,
Calle Coso Viejo (tel: 84 21 80).
Aracena: Plaza San Pedro (tel:
(955) 11 03 55).
Arcos de la Frontera: Cuesta de
Beten (tel: (956) 70 22 64).
Cádiz: Calle Calderón de la
Barca 1 (tel: (956) 21 13 13); Calle
Marqués de Valde-Iñigo 4 (tel:
(956) 25 32 54).
Carmona: Plaza de las Descalzas
(tel: (95) 414 2200).
Córdoba: Calle Torijos 10 (tel: 47
12 35); Ayuntamiento, Plaza de
Judas (tel: (957) 47 20 00).
Ecija: Avenida de Andalucía

Late night revelry Seville-style

(tel: 438 30 62).
Estepa: Plaza del Carmen 1 (tel:
482 10 00).
Granada: Calle Libreros 2 (tel:
(958) 22 10 22).
Huelva: Avenida de Alemania 1
(tel: (955) 25 74 03).
Jerez de la Frontera: Alameda
Cristina 7 (tel: (956) 33 11 50).
Matalascañas: Urbanizacion
Playa de Matalascañas (tel: (955)
43 00 86).
Mazagón: Edificio
Mancommunidad Moguer-Palos,
(tel: (955) 37 60 44).
Osuna: Casa de la Cultura, Calle
Sevilla 22 (tel: (95) 481 22 11);
Museo Arqueológico, Calle San
Antón (tel: (95) 481 12 07).
Palos de la Frontera: Acceso al
Complejo de La Rábida (tel:
(955) 35 12 58).
El Puerto de Santa María: Calle
Guadalete (tel: (956) 85 75 45).

LANGUAGE

Andalucians speak Castilian, the 'standard' Spanish. Words are often similar to those of other European languages, especially French and Italian. The hardest part is learning the pronunciation. The main rules are given here. One thing to beware of: many Andalucians pronounce 'c' and 'z' like a hard 's' sound, instead of the usual lisping 'th' (see below). They may also clip the ends of their words and talk rapidly.

Pronunciation

a—as in tar
e—as in let
i—as in marine
o—as in Tom
u—as in rule
b and **v**—similar, like a soft 'b'
c—like 'th' in thin before 'e' or 'i'; otherwise as in cat
g—like 'ch' in loch before 'e' or 'i'; otherwise as in get
j—like 'ch' in loch
ll—like 'lli' in million
ñ—like 'ni' in onion
r—strong and rolled, **rr** more so
z—like 'th' in thin

Stress

Stress the second-to-last syllable if the word ends in n, s, or a vowel. This means nearly all words. Other words have the stress on the last syllable, like Madrid, or wherever there is an accent, as in Málaga and Córdoba.

Useful words and phrases

hello hola
I am sorry, but I don't speak Spanish lo siento, pero no hablo español
do you speak English? habla inglés?
is there someone who speaks ... ? hay alguien que hable ...
yes/no si/no
excuse me, I don't understand perdón, no comprendo
please speak slowly por favor, hable despacio
thank you (very much) (muchas) gracias
you're welcome/think nothing of it de nada
good morning buenos días
good afternoon buenas tardes
good evening buenas noches
I am/my name is ... soy/me llamo ...
what is your name? como se llama usted?
how are you? como está?
I am ... estoy ...
very well muy bien
I (don't) know (something) (no) sé
I (don't) know (a person) (no) conozco
all right vale/de acuerdo
good luck buena suerte
goodbye adiós
see you again hasta luego
where is ...? donde está?
is it far/near? está lejos/cerca?
very muy
left/right/ahead/at the end izquierda/derecha/delante/ al final
avenue/boulevard/road/street/ passage/square avenida/ paseo/carretera/calle/pasaje/ plaça
countryside/mountain (mountains)/hill/river/stream campo/montaña (sierra)/ colina/río/arroyo
castle/church/monastery/palace/ school castillo/iglesia/ monasterio/palacio/escuela
open/closed abierto/cerrado
hour/day/week/month/year hora/día/semana/mes/año

Monday to Sunday lunes, martes, miercoles, jueves, viernes, sábado, domingo
yesterday/today/tomorrow ayer/hoy/mañana
last night/tonight anoche/esta noche
the weekend el fin de semana
last week/next week semana pasada/semana próxima
early/late temprano/tarde
I would like ... me gustaría ...
do you have ...? tiene ...?
there is (not) (no) hay
how much is? cuánto es/vale/cuesta?
expensive/cheap caro/barato
short/long corto/largo

enough/too much bastante/demasiado
more/less más/menos
good/better bueno/mejor
big/bigger grande/más grande
small/smaller pequeño/más pequeño
nothing more nada más
Numbers
1 to 10 uno, dos, tres, cuatro, cinco, seis, siete, ocho, nueve, diez
11 to 19 once, doce, trece, catorce, quince, dieciseis, diecisiete, dieciocho, diecinueve
20 to 100 veinte, trienta, cuarenta, cincuenta, sesenta, setenta, ochenta, noventa, cien, doscientos
500 quinientos
1,000 mil

Plaza de España's decorative tiles

INDEX/ACKNOWLEDGEMENTS

The Automobile Association wishes to thank the following photographers and libraries for their assistance in the preparation of this book.

ANDREW MOLYNEUX took all the photographs (© AA PHOTO LIBRARY) except:

J ALLAN CASH PHOTOLIBRARY 75 Cabo de Trafalgar.

MARY EVANS PICTURE LIBRARY 15 Columbus.

NATURE PHOTOGRAPHERS LTD 71 Sea holly (R O Bush), 72/3 Bee-eater (K J Carlson), 76 Flamingo (H Clark).

SPECTRUM COLOUR LIBRARY Cover Plaza de España.

WORLD PICTURES 5 Parque de María Luisa, 55 Antequera, 57 Arcos de la Frontera, 60/1 Córdoba Mosque, 64 Granada Alhambra, 67/8 Jerez Fair of the Horse, 110 National Costume.